I0428282

ENGLISH LANGUAGE IN A MULTILINGUAL SOCIETY:
ITS INFLUENCE ON NIGERIAN LANGUAGES AND CULTURES.

(A CASE STUDY OF REDEEMERS UNIVERSITY, MOWE, OGUN STATE, NIGERIA.)

RESEARCHER: DR. JANE OLAMIDE LANDEY

Copyright©2014

All rights reserved.

ISBN-13: 978-1500686956

Printed in U.S.A.

ACKNOWLEDGEMENTS

English Language in a Multilingual Society: Its Influence on Nigerian Languages and Cultures is the topic of the research work that was carried out in the Department of English, Redeemers University, Mowe, Ogun State, Nigeria between March 2012 to 2013 though extended to 2014. All of the gratitude go to the Vice Chancellor Prof. Z.D. Adeyewa,who gave his approval and my mentor, Prof. Funsho Akere, the Head of Department, English, who helped in commencing the research smoothly. They were the hand work of this piece of work because without their permission it would not have come to the lime light..

Dr. Adebola Adebileje, my advisor and supervisor, was of great help and assistant to the core. The secretary to the Head of Department English, Mrs. Joy Ocholi was my companion and a person who uplifted my spirit. Mr. Samson Olugbenga John, the Chief Security Officer, assigned to protect me and guide my activities expressed great concern and care to the core.

The research began smoothly with the use of the university library and information from my supervisor, Dr, Adebola Adebileje and these paved way for successful contribution. Students in three hundred level taking the course of Dr. Adebola Adebileje which was related to the research topic provided adequate information in the questionnaires given to them.

During the course of the research, a trip to Germany, University of Hamburg, gave me the opportunity to meet Mr. Micah Corum,

 Mr. Richard Bonnie and Miss Daniella Schroeder who were lecturers in the Department on English. They released their students to fill the questionnaires on the research , thus giving me the ideas on the interference between German and English languages. This also helped the conclusion of the research.

Mrs. Grace A. Odetunde of the Ministry of Education District 1 Agege, Lagos State, was most helpful financially.

Introduction

The question as to the number of <u>indigenous languages</u> Nigerians use along with English has not been resolved. This, <u>according</u>

<u>to</u> Emenanjo (1990: vi), is because "Nigeria is a classical <u>multilingual</u> mosaic in which minority languages, which are very many in number, live cheek-by-jowl with major languages which, at a micro level, are only three in number or, at a macro level, are nine or twelve in number." However, this paper considers both "major" and "minor" languages as Nigerian indigenous languages. While the Federal Government, in its language policy, has <u>categorised</u> three (Hausa, Yoruba and Igbo) as "major" languages out of over four

hundred Nigerian local languages, Williamson (1990) made a brilliant list of 118 "minority" languages which have been found to have <u>determinate</u> geography and speakers as well as literature and potentials of being developed. In addition to the above languages, there must be other local languages spoken largely in some rural areas of the country, which have not yet been "discovered". And of course, there is the <u>English language</u>, which at present functions together with the so-called major Nigerian languages as the national language of the country. But the position, which English occupies in the country, is unique, though it does not function as a vehicle for expressing the indigenous cultures.

The exact number of Nigerian indigenous languages is not important in this paper. What is important is the influence of English Language on our local languages and cultures.

Language has been described as a vehicle for thought (Sapir 1929). And a nation's culture is largely reflected through the thoughts of its people. So for a culture to remain alive, the language(s) through which it is transmitted should be preserved. Language again powerfully conditions all our thinking about social problems and processes (Sapir 1929; Whorf 1974). Social problems confronting the communities are also solved through language. In fact, it is as a vehicle of culture that language functions as an instrument of human development. In Akindele and Adegbite's (1992: 6) view, "the individual's experience of reality is functionally dependent upon the language and linguistic behavior of a given society". We therefore submit in this paper that the Nigerian indigenous languages should not be treated with scorn, but be accorded respect in line with their significant role of preserving the indigenous cultures. It is a known fact that English is a national language of the country, but the indigenous culture cannot be reflected or preserved through it. This is because English is a foreign language and no amount of <u>domestication</u> can make it adequately reflect Nigeria's diverse traditional beliefs, norms, arts, etc. It has been observed that there are many instances of the physical environment of a society being reflected in its language, normally in the structure of its lexicon -- the way in which distinctions are made by means of single words (Trudgill 1971).

Culture, according to Onwuanibe (1980: 61), is: "The ensemble of activities of state of a people's development with regard to intellectual, aesthetic, religious, moral, scientific and technical achievements, and the environment which furthers them from man's creative spirit as he poses and endeavors to answer questions around and beyond himself. It is man's way of life as he meets his physical and spiritual needs."

Therefore, the multilingual and multicultural nature of the country should be seen as a blessing rather than a curse since the rich diverse cultures will make the country <u>impervious</u> to erosion from foreign cultural influences that may be <u>inimical</u> to her moral values and national interest. Countries all over the world are turning back to their rich cultural heritage with a view to exporting the best aspects to generate foreign currency. Nigeria cannot be an exception. Thus, a country like Nigeria with relatively few of her citizens literate in English cannot toy with the idea of seeking to replace all the indigenous languages with the English language whose native speakers' culture remains largely <u>esoteric</u> and foreign. From the foregoing, it is imperative that these languages be developed in order to keep alive the cultures they project. A nation that watches its language die is at the same time killing its culture. And when a nation loses its culture, it may no longer have a basis for existence. Onwuanibe (1980) contends that technology is part of culture and that a nation with a <u>virile</u> culture is just an inch away from being a superpower in the world of technology. He explains that while culture is a holistic phenomenon, technology refers to man as a tool-making creature. By helping man to control nature, thereby helping man to maintain and enhance the quality of his life, technology is an indispensable part of culture. We may then say that Nigeria remains a technologically backward nation, not because it has not recorded any feat in the field of technology, but because it lacks developed indigenous language(s) through which its technological feats could be recorded, processed and transmitted to the world at large. What the country should do to make her impact felt in the technological world is to nurture its indigenous languages so that her technological feats being expressed in a foreign language will be saved from international pilfering. After all, Japan, for example, is today a technological giant as a result of the promotion of its indigenous language through which her technology is sold to the world. Given that some of the Nigerian indigenous languages, which include the so-called major ones, have been developed to some extent with regard to orthography, the government should act decisively and map out standardisation strategies for these languages. Emenanjo (1990) states that work on the writing systems for Nigerian languages must be carefully and democratically carried out at the local and/or state levels before such systems can be standardised and made official by the National Language Centre (NLC).

The government itself has acknowledged the importance of a language in the preservation of the peoples' culture (NPE: [section]8). The development and preservation of these languages, as a way of preserving the national heritage is very imperative. According to Linton (1947), "The culture of a society is the way of life of its members; the collection of ideas and habits which they learn, share and transmit from generation to generation. To a large degree, culture determines how member of a society think and feel; it directs their actions and defines their outlook."

We acquire knowledge of the social and cultural values of our societies through languages in which such social and cultural values are preserved. The loss of these languages will mean the loss of such values. Also, the constraints, which the society imposes on behaviour, including language behaviour, are some of the societal norms and values that are preserved in our indigenous languages. Another area of a symbiotic relationship between language and culture is taboo. According to Akindele and Adegbite (1992), taboo is associated with things, which are not said, or in particular with words and expressions which are not used. The types of words that are tabooed in a particular language are a reflection of at least part of the system of values and beliefs of the society in question.
The local councils which form the third tier in the government system

and which are closer enough to the rural people where most of the indigenous languages are spoken are in the best position to know these languages, to identify and assemble them through the cooperation of the local populace. Developmental tasks can then be mapped out for the languages by the appropriate authorities within the local councils.

Contents

Geographical, Historical and Cultural Patterns of Nigeria

Culture Name

Nigerian

Orientation

Identification. Though there is archaeological evidence that societies have been living in Nigeria for more than twenty-five hundred years, the borders of modern Nigeria were not created until the British consolidated their colonial power over the area in 1914.

The name Nigeria was suggested by British journalist Flora Shaw in the 1890s. She referred to the area as Nigeria, after the Niger River, which dominates much of the country's landscape. The word *niger* is Latin for black.

More than 250 ethnic tribes call present-day Nigeria home. The three largest and most dominant ethnic groups are the Hausa, Yoruba, and Igbo (pronounced ee-bo). Other smaller groups include the Fulani, Ijaw, Kanuri, Ibibio, Tiv, and Edo. Prior to their conquest by Europeans, these ethnic groups had separate and independent histories. Their grouping together into a single entity known as Nigeria was a construct of their British colonizers. These various ethnic groups never considered themselves part of the same culture. This general lack of Nigerian nationalism coupled with an ever-changing and often ethnically biased national leadership, have led to severe internal ethnic conflicts and a civil war. Today bloody confrontations between or among members of different ethnic groups continue.

Location and Geography. Nigeria is in West Africa, along the eastern coast of the Gulf of Guinea, and just north of the equator. It is bordered on the west by Benin, on the north by Niger and Chad, and on the east by Cameroon. Nigeria covers an area of 356,669 square miles (923,768 square kilometers), or about twice the size of California.

Nigeria has three main environmental regions: savanna, tropical forests, and coastal wetlands. These environmental regions greatly affect the cultures of the people who live there. The dry, open grasslands of the savanna make cereal farming and herding a way of life for the Hausa and the Fulani. The wet tropical forests to the south are good for farming fruits and vegetables—main income producers for the Yoruba, Igbo, and others in this area. The small ethnic groups living along the coast, such as the Ijaw and the Kalabari, are forced to keep their villages small due to lack of dry land. Living among creeks, lagoons, and salt marshes makes fishing and the salt trade part of everyday life in the area.

The Niger and Benue Rivers come together in the center of the country, creating a "Y" that splits Nigeria into three separate sections. In general, this "Y" marks the boundaries of the three major ethnic groups, with the Hausa in the north, the Yoruba in the southwest, and the Igbo in the southeast.

Politically, Nigeria is divided into thirty-six states. The nation's capital was moved from Lagos, the country's largest city, to Abuja on 12 December 1991. Abuja is in a federal territory that is not part of any state. While Abuja is the official capital, its lack of adequate infrastructure means that Lagos remains the financial, commercial, and diplomatic center of the country.

Demography. Nigeria has the largest population of any African country. In July 2000, Nigeria's population was estimated at more than 123 million people. At about 345 people per square mile, it is also the most densely populated country in Africa. Nearly one in six Africans is a Nigerian. Despite the rampages of AIDS, Nigeria's population continues to grow at about 2.6 percent each year. The Nigerian population is very young. Nearly 45 percent of its people are under age fourteen.

With regard to ethnic breakdown, the Hausa-Fulani make up 29 percent of the population, followed by the Yoruba with 21 percent, the Igbo with

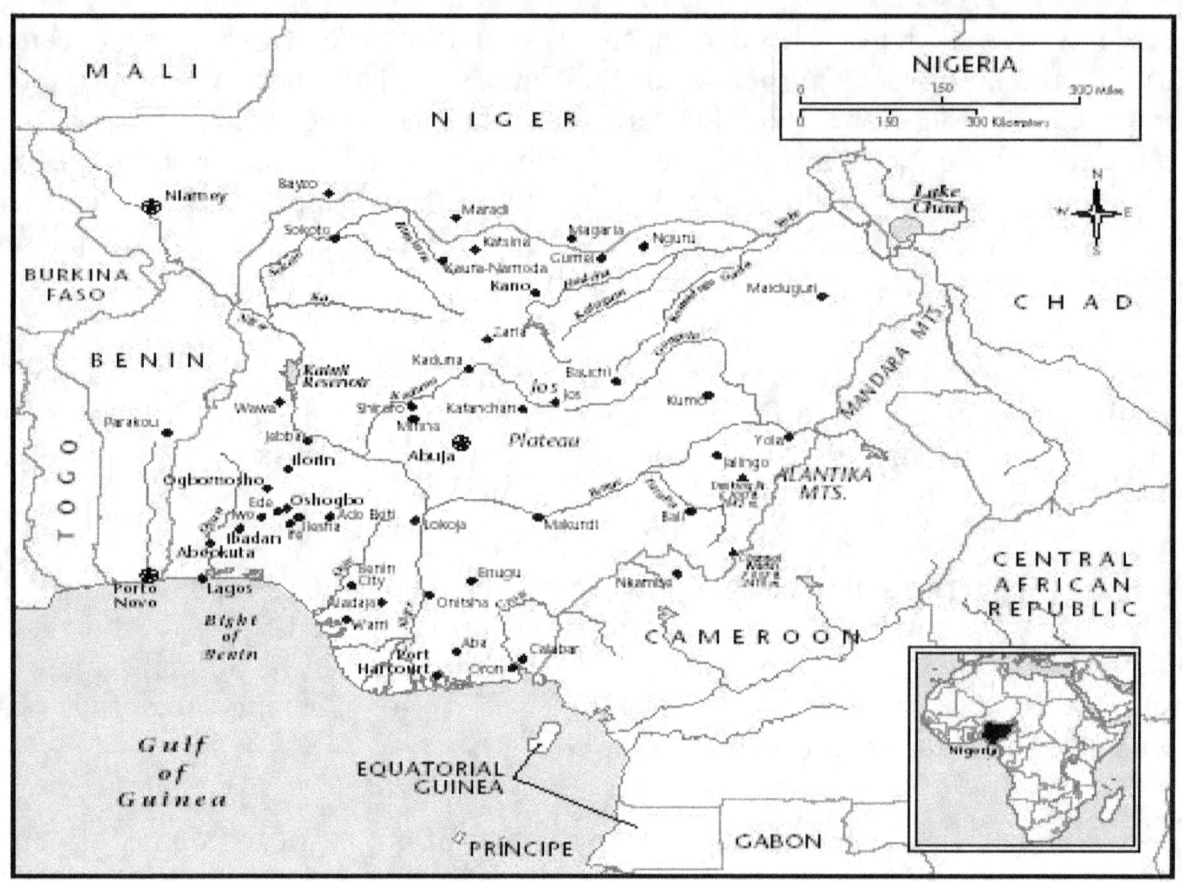

Nigeria

18 percent, the Ijaw with 10 percent, the Kanuri with 4 percent, the Ibibio with 3.5 percent, and the Tiv with 2.5 percent.

Major urban centers include Lagos, Ibidan, Kaduna, Kano, and Port Harcourt.

Linguistic Affiliations. English is the official language of Nigeria, used in all government interactions and in state-run schools. In a country with more than 250 individual tribal languages, English is the only language common to most people.

Unofficially, the country's second language is Hausa. In northern Nigeria many people who are not ethnic Hausas speak both Hausa and their own tribal language. Hausa is the oldest known written language in West Africa, dating back to before 1000 C.E.

The dominant indigenous languages of the south are Yoruba and Igbo. Prior to colonization, these languages were the unifying languages of the southwest and southeast, respectively, regardless of ethnicity. However, since the coming of the

British and the introduction of mission schools in southern Nigeria, English has become the language common to most people in the area. Today those who are not ethnic Yorubas or Igbos rarely speak Yoruba or Igbo.

Pidgin, a mix of African languages and English, also is common throughout southern Nigeria. It basically uses English words mixed into Yoruban or Igbo grammar structures. Pidgin originally evolved from the need for British sailors to find a way to communicate with local merchants. Today it is often used in ethnically mixed urban areas as a common form of communication among people who have not had formal education in English.

Symbolism. Because there is little feeling of national unity among Nigeria's people, there is little in terms of national symbolism. What exists was usually created or unveiled by the government as representative of the nation. The main national symbol is the country's flag. The flag is divided vertically into three equal parts; the center section is white, flanked by two green sections. The green of the flag represents agriculture, while the white stands for unity and peace. Other national symbols include the national coat of arms, the national anthem, the National Pledge (similar to the Pledge of Allegiance in the United States), and Nigeria's national motto: Peace and Unity, Strength and Progress.

History and Ethnic Relations

Emergence of the Nation. Every ethnic group in Nigeria has its own stories of where its ancestors came from. These vary from tales of people descending from the sky to stories of migration from far-off places. Archaeologists have found evidence of Neolithic humans who inhabited what is now Nigeria as far back as 12,000 B.C.E.

The histories of the people in northern and southern Nigeria prior to colonization followed vastly different paths. The first recorded empire in present-day Nigeria was centered in the north at Kanem-Borno, near Lake Chad. This empire came to power during the eighth century C.E. By the thirteenth century, many Hausa states began to emerge in the region as well.

Trans-Sahara trade with North Africans and Arabs began to transform these northern societies greatly. Increased contact with the Islamic world led to the conversion of the Kanem-Borno Empire to Islam in the eleventh century. This led to a ripple effect of conversions throughout the north. Islam brought with it changes in law, education, and politics.

The trans-Sahara trade also brought with it revolutions in wealth and class structure. As the centuries went on, strict Islamists, many of whom were poor Fulani, began to tire of increasing corruption, excessive taxation, and unfair treatment of the poor. In 1804 the Fulani launched a jihad, or Muslim holy war, against the Hausa states in an attempt to cleanse them of these non-Muslim behaviors and to reintroduce proper Islamic ways. By 1807 the last Hausa state had fallen. The Fulani victors founded the Sokoto Caliphate, which grew to become the largest state in West Africa until its conquest by the British in 1903.

In the south, the Oyo Empire grew to become the most powerful Yoruban society during the sixteenth century. Along the coast, the Edo people established the Benin Empire (not to be confused with the present-day country of Benin to the west), which reached its height of power in the fifteenth and sixteenth centuries.

As in the north, outsiders heavily influenced the societies of southern Nigeria. Contact with Europeans began with the arrival of Portuguese ships in 1486. The British, French, and Dutch soon followed. Soon after their arrival, the trade in slaves replaced the original trade in goods. Many of the coastal communities began selling their neighbors, whom they had captured in wars and raids, to the Europeans in exchange for things such as guns, metal, jewelry, and liquor.

The slave trade had major social consequences for the Africans. Violence and intertribal warfare increased as the search for slaves intensified. The increased wealth accompanying the slave trade began to change social structures in the area. Leadership, which had been based on tradition and ritual, soon became based on wealth and economic power.

After more than 350 years of slave trading, the British decided that the slave trade was immoral and, in 1807, ordered it stopped. They began to force their newfound morality on the Nigerians. Many local leaders, however, continued to sell captives to illegal slave traders. This lead to confrontations with the British Navy, which took on the responsibility of enforcing the slave embargo. In 1851 the British attacked Lagos to try to stem the flow of slaves from the area. By 1861 the British government had annexed the city and established its first official colony in Nigeria.

As the non-slave trade began to flourish, so, too, did the Nigerian economy. A new economy based on raw materials, agricultural products, and locally manufactured goods saw the growth of a new class of Nigerian merchants. These merchants were heavily influenced by Western ways. Many soon became involved in politics, often criticizing chiefs for keeping to their traditional ways. A new divide within

Central Ibadan, the second-largest city. Nigeria is the most densely populated country in Africa.

the local communities began to develop, in terms of both wealth and politics. Because being a successful merchant was based on production and merit, not on traditional community standing, many former slaves and lower-class people soon found that they could advance quickly up the social ladder. It was not unusual to find a former slave transformed into the richest, most powerful man in the area.

Christian missionaries brought Western-style education to Nigeria as Christianity quickly spread throughout the south. The mission schools created an educated African elite who also sought increased contact with Europe and a Westernization of Nigeria.

In 1884, as European countries engaged in a race to consolidate their African territories, the British Army and local merchant militias set out to conquer the Africans who refused to recognize British rule. In 1914, after squelching the last of the indigenous opposition, Britain officially established the Colony and Protectorate of Nigeria.

National Identity. The spread of overt colonial control led to the first and only time that the ethnic groups in modern Nigeria came together under a commonly felt sense of national identity. The Africans began to see themselves not as Hausas, Igbos, or Yorubas, but as Nigerians in a common struggle against their colonial rulers.

The nationalistic movement grew out of some of the modernization the British had instituted in Nigeria. The educated elite became some of the most outspoken proponents of an independent Nigeria. This elite had grown weary of the harsh racism it faced in business and administrative jobs within the government. Both the elite and the uneducated also began to grow fearful of the increasing loss of traditional culture. They began movements to promote Nigerian foods, names, dress, languages, and religions.

Increased urbanization and higher education brought large multiethnic groups together for the first time. As a result of this coming together, the Nigerians saw that they had more in common with each other than they had previously thought. This sparked unprecedented levels of interethnic teamwork. Nigerian political movements, media outlets, and trade unions whose purpose was the advancement of all Nigerians, not specific ethnic groups, became commonplace.

As calls for self-determination and a transfer of power into the hands of Nigerians grew, Britain began to divest more power into the regional governments. As a result of early colonial policies of divide and conquer, the regional governments tended to be drawn along ethnic lines. With this move to greater regional autonomy, the idea of a unified Nigeria became to crumble. Regionally and ethnically based political parties sprang up as ethnic groups began to wrangle for political influence.

Ethnic Relations. Nigeria gained full independence from Britain on 1 October 1960. Immediately following independence, vicious fighting between and among political parties created chaos within the fledgling democracy. On 15 January 1966 a group of army officers, most of whom were Igbo, staged a military coup, killing many of the government ministers from the western and northern tribes. Six months later, northern forces within the military staged a countercoup, killing most of the Igbo leaders. Anti-Igbo demonstrations broke out across the country, especially in the north. Hundreds of Igbos were killed, while the rest fled to the southeast.

On 26 May 1967 the Igbo-dominated southeast declared it had broken away from Nigeria to form the independent Republic of Biafra. This touched off a bloody civil war that lasted for three years. In 1970, on the brink of widespread famine resulting from a Nigeria-imposed blockade, Biafra was forced to surrender. Between five hundred thousand and two million Biafran civilians were killed during the civil war, most dying from starvation, not combat.

Following the war, the military rulers encouraged a national reconciliation, urging Nigerians to once again become a unified people. While this national reconciliation succeeded in reintegrating the Biafrans into Nigeria, it did not end the problems of ethnicity in the country. In the years that followed, Nigeria was continually threatened by disintegration due to ethnic fighting. These ethnic conflicts reached their height in the 1990s.

After decades of military rule, elections for a new civilian president were finally held on 12 June 1993. A wealthy Yoruba Muslim named Moshood Abiola won the elections, beating the leading Hausa candidate. Abiola won support not only from his own people but from many non-Yorubas as well, including many Hausas. This marked the first time since Nigeria's independence that Nigerians broke from ethnically based voting practices. Two weeks later, however, the military regime had the election results annulled and Abiola imprisoned. Many commanders in the Hausa-dominated military feared losing control to a southerner. They played on the nation's old ethnic distrusts, hoping that a divided nation would be easier to control. This soon created a new ethnic crisis. The next five years saw violent protests and mass migrations as ethnic groups again retreated to their traditional homelands.

The sudden death of Nigeria's last military dictator, General Suni Abacha, on 8 June 1998 opened the door for a transition back to civilian rule. Despite age-old ethnic rivalries, many Nigerians again crossed ethnic lines when they entered the voting booth. On 22 February 1999 Olusegun Obasanjo, a Yoruba who ironically lacked support from his own people, won the presidential election. Obasanjo is seen as a nationalist who opposed ethnic divisions. However, some northern leaders believe he favors his own ethnic group.

Unfortunately, violent ethnic fighting in Nigeria continues. In October 2000, clashes between Hausas and supporters of the Odua People's Congress (OPC), a militant Yoruba group, led to the deaths of nearly a hundred people in Lagos. Many also blame the OPC for sparking riots in 1999, which killed more than a hundred others, most of them Hausas.

Urbanism, Architecture, and the Use of Space

With the influx of oil revenue and foreigners, Nigerian cities have grown to resemble many Western urban centers. Lagos, for example, is a massive, overcrowded city filled with traffic jams, movie theaters, department stores, restaurants, and supermarkets. Because most Nigerian cities grew out of much older towns, very little urban planning was used as the cities expanded. Streets are laid out in a confusing and often mazelike fashion, adding to the chaos for pedestrians and traffic. The influx of people into urban areas has put a strain on many services. Power cuts and disruptions of telephone service are not uncommon.

Nigerian architecture is as diverse as its people. In rural areas, houses often are designed to accommodate the environment in which the people live. The Ijo live in the Niger Delta region, where dry land is very scarce. To compensate for this, many Ijo homes are built on stilts over creeks and swamps, with travel between them done by boat. The houses are made of wood and bamboo and topped with a roof made of fronds from raffia palms. The houses are very airy, to allow heat and the smoke from cooking fires to escape easily.

Igbo houses tend to be made of a bamboo frame held together with vines and mud and covered with banana leaves. They often blend into the surrounding forest and can be easily missed if you don't know where to look. Men and women traditionally live in separate houses.

Much of the architecture in the north is heavily influenced by Muslim culture. Homes are typically geometric, mud-walled structures, often with Muslim markings and decorations. The Hausa build large, walled compounds housing several smaller huts. The entryway into the compound is via a large hut built into the wall of the compound. This is the hut of the father or head male figure in the compound.

Food and Economy

Read more about the <u>Food and Cuisine of Nigeria</u>.

Food in Daily Life. Western influences, especially in urban centers, have transformed Nigerian eating habits in many ways. City dwellers are familiar with the canned, frozen, and prepackaged foods found in most Western-style supermarkets. Foreign restaurants also are common in larger cities. However, supermarkets and restaurants often are too expensive for the average Nigerian; thus only the wealthy can afford to eat like Westerners. Most urban Nigerians seem to combine traditional cuisine with a little of Western-style foods and conveniences. Rural Nigerians tend to stick more with traditional foods and preparation techniques.

Food in Nigeria is traditionally eaten by hand. However, with the growing influence of Western culture, forks and spoons are becoming more common, even in remote villages. Whether people eat with their hand or a utensil, it is considered dirty and rude to eat using the left hand.

While the ingredients in traditional plates vary from region to region, most Nigerian cuisine tends to be based around a few staple foods accompanied by a stew. In the south, crops such as corn, yams, and sweet potatoes form the base of the diet. These vegetables are often pounded into a thick, sticky dough or paste. This is often served with a palm oil based stew made with chicken, beef, goat, tomatoes, okra, onions, bitter leaves, or whatever meats and vegetables might be on hand. Fruits such as papaya, pineapples, coconuts, oranges, mangoes, and bananas also are very common in the tropical south.

In the north, grains such as millet, sorghum, and corn are boiled into a porridge-like dish that forms the basis of the diet. This is served with an oil based soup usually flavored with onions, okra, and tomatoes. Sometimes meat is included, though among the Hausa it is often reserved for special occasions. Thanks to the Fulani cattle herders, fresh milk and yogurt are common even though there may not be refrigeration.

Alcohol is very popular in the south but less so in the north, where there is a heavy Islamic influence. Perhaps the most popular form of alcohol is palm wine, a tart alcoholic drink that comes from palm trees. Palm wine is often distilled further to make a strong, gin like liquor. Nigerian breweries also produce several kinds of beer and liquor.

Food Customs at Ceremonial Occasions. Food plays a central role in the rituals of virtually all ethnic groups in Nigeria. Special ceremonies would not be complete without participants sharing in a meal. Normally it is considered rude not to invite guests to share in a meal when they visit; it is even more so if the visitors were invited to attend a special event such as a marriage or a naming ceremony.

Basic Economy. Until the past few decades, Nigeria had been self-sufficient in producing enough food to feed the population. However, as petroleum production and industry began to boom in Nigeria, much of the national resources were concentrated on the new industries at the expense of agriculture.

Nigeria, which had previously been a net exporter of agricultural products, soon needed to import vast amounts of food it once was able to produce for itself.

Since the 1960s, Nigeria's economy has been based on oil production. As a leading member of the Organization of Petroleum Exporting Countries (OPEC), Nigeria has played a major role in influencing the price of oil on the world market. The oil-rich economy led to a major economic boom for Nigeria during the 1970s, transforming the poor African country into the thirtieth richest country in the world. However, falling oil prices, severe corruption, political instability, and economic mismanagement since then have left Nigeria no better off today than it was at independence.

Since the restoration of civilian rule in 1999, Nigeria has begun to make strides in economic reform. While hopes are high for a strong economic transformation, high unemployment, high inflation, and more than a third of the population living under the poverty line indicate it will be a long and difficult road.

Oil production has had some long-lasting ethnic consequences as well. While oil is Nigeria's largest industry in terms of output and revenue, oil reserves are found only in the Niger Delta region and along the coast. The government has long taken the oil revenues and dispersed them throughout the country. In this way, states not involved in oil production still get a share of the profits. This has led to claims that the minority ethnic groups living in the delta are being cheated out of revenue that is rightfully theirs because the larger ethnic groups dominate politics. Sometimes this has led to large-scale violence.

More than 50 percent of Nigeria's population works in the agriculture sector. Most farmers engage in subsistence farming, producing only what they eat themselves or sell locally. Very few agricultural products are produced for export.

Land Tenure and Property. While the federal government has the legal right to allocate land as it sees fit, land tenure remains largely a local issue. Most local governments follow traditional land tenure customs in their areas. For example, in Hausa society, title to land is not an absolute right. While communities and officials will honor long-standing hereditary rights to areas of land traditionally claimed by a given family, misused or abandoned land may be reapportioned for better use. Land also can be bought, sold, or rented. In the west, the Yoruban kings historically held all the land in trust, and therefore also had a say in how it was used for the good of the community. This has given local governments in modern times a freer hand in settling land disputes.

Traditionally, only men hold land, but as the wealth structure continues to change and develop in Nigeria, it would not be unheard of for a wealthy woman to purchase land for herself.

Major Industries. Aside from petroleum and petroleum-based products, most of the goods produced in Nigeria are consumed within Nigeria. For example, though the textile industry is very strong, nearly all the cloth produced in Nigeria goes to clothing the large Nigerian population.

Major agricultural products produced in Nigeria include cocoa, peanuts, palm oil, rice, millet, corn, cassava, yams, rubber, cattle, sheep, goats, pigs, timber, and fish. Major commercial industries in Nigeria include coal, tin, textiles, footwear, fertilizer, printing, ceramics, and steel.

Trade. Oil and petroleum-based products made up 95 percent of Nigeria's exports in 1998. Cocoa and rubber are also produced for export. Major export partners include the United States, Spain, India, France, and Italy.

Nigeria is a large-scale importer, depending on other countries for things such as machinery, chemicals, transportation equipment, and manufactured goods. The country also must import large quantities of food and livestock. Major import partners include the United Kingdom, the United States, Germany, France, and the Netherlands.

Social Stratification

Classes and Castes. The highest tier of Nigerian society is made up of wealthy politicians, businessmen, and the educated elite. These people, however, make up only a tiny portion of the Nigerian population. Many Nigerians today suffer under great poverty. The lower classes tend have little chance of breaking from the vicious cycle of poverty. Poor education, lack of opportunities, ill health, corrupt politicians, and lack of even small amounts of wealth for investment all work to keep the lower classes in their place.

In some Nigerian ethnic groups there is also a form of caste system that treats certain members of society as pariahs. The criteria for determining who belongs to this lowest caste vary from area to area but can include being a member of a minority group, an inhabitant of a specific village, or a member of a specific family or clan. The Igbo call this lower-caste group Osu. Members of the community will often discourage personal, romantic, and business contact with any member of the Osu group, regardless of an individual's personal merits or characteristics. Because the Osu are designated as untouchable, they often lack political representation, access to basic educational or business opportunities, and general social interaction. This kind of caste system is also found among the Yoruba and the Ibibios.

Symbols of Social Stratification. Wealth is the main symbol of social stratification in modern Nigeria, especially in urban areas. While in the past many ethnic groups held hereditary titles and traditional lineage important, money has become the new marker of power and social status. Today the members of the wealthy elite are easily identifiable by their fancy clothing and hairstyles and by their expensive cars and Western-style homes. Those in the elite also tend to have a much better command of English, a reflection of the higher quality of education they have received.

A man places skewers of meat in a circle around a fire. Rural Nigerians favor traditional foods and preparation techniques.

Wealth also can be important in marking social boundaries in rural areas. In many ethnic groups, those who have accumulated enough wealth can buy themselves local titles. For example, among the Igbo, a man or a woman who has enough money may claim the title of *Ozo.* For women, one of the requirements to become an *Ozo* is to have enough ivory, coral, and other jewelry for the ceremony. The weight of the jewelry can often exceed fifty pounds. Both men and women who want to claim the title must also finance a feast for the entire community.

Political Life

Government. Nigeria is a republic, with the president acting as both head of state and head of government. Nigeria has had a long history of *coups d'états,* military rule, and dictatorship. However, this pattern was broken on 29 May 1999 as Nigeria's current president, Olusegun Obasanjo, took office following popular elections. Under the current constitution, presidential elections are to be held every four years, with no president serving more than two terms in office. The Nigerian legislature consists of two houses: a Senate and a House of Representatives. All legislators are elected to four-year terms. Nigeria's judicial branch is headed by a Supreme Court, whose members were appointed by the Provisional Ruling Council, which ruled Nigeria during its recent transition to democracy. All Nigerians over age eighteen are eligible to vote.

Leadership and Political Officials. A wealthy political elite dominates political life in Nigeria. The relationship between the political elite and ordinary Nigerians is not unlike that between nobles and commoners. Nigerian leaders, whether as members of a military regime or one of Nigeria's short-lived civilian governments, have a history of doing whatever it takes to stay in power and to hold on to the wealth that this power has given them.

Rural Nigerians tend to accept this noble-peasant system of politics. Low levels of education and literacy mean that many people in rural areas are not fully aware of the political process or how to affect it. Their relative isolation from the rest of the country means that many do not even think of politics. There is a common feeling in many rural areas that the average person cannot affect the politics of the country, so there is no reason to try.

Urban Nigerians tend to be much more vocal in their support of or opposition to their leaders. Urban problems of housing, unemployment, health care, sanitation, and traffic tend to mobilize people into political action and public displays of dissatisfaction.

Political parties were outlawed under the Abacha regime, and only came back into being after his death. As of the 1999 presidential elections, there were three main political parties in Nigeria: the People's Democratic Party (PDP), the All Peoples Party (APP), and the Alliance for Democracy (AD). The PDP is the party of President Obasanjo. It grew out of support for opposition leaders who were imprisoned by the military government in the early 1990s. The PDP is widely believed to have received heavy financial assistance from the military during the 1999 elections. The APP is led by politicians who had close ties to the Abacha regime. The AD is a party led by followers of the late Moshood Abiola, the Yoruba politician who won the general election in 1993, only to be sent to prison by the military regime.

Social Problems and Control. Perhaps Nigeria's greatest social problem is the internal violence plaguing the nation. Interethnic fighting throughout the country, religious rioting between Muslims and non-Muslims over the creation of Shari'a law (strict Islamic law) in the northern states, and political confrontations between ethnic minorities and backers of oil companies often spark bloody confrontations that can last days or even months. When violence of this type breaks out, national and state police try to control it. However, the police themselves are often accused of some of the worst violence. In some instances, curfews and martial law have been imposed in specific areas to try to stem outbreaks of unrest.

Poverty and lack of opportunity for many young people, especially in urban areas, have led to major crime. Lagos is considered one of the most dangerous cities in West Africa due to its incredibly high crime rate. The police are charged with controlling crime, but their lack of success often leads to vigilante justice.

In some rural areas there are some more traditional ways of addressing social problems. In many ethnic groups, such as the Igbo and the Yoruba, men are organized into secret societies. Initiated members of these societies often dress in masks and palm leaves to masquerade as the physical embodiment of traditional spirits to help maintain social order. Through ritual dance, these men will give warnings about problems with an individual's or community's morality in a given situation. Because belief in witchcraft and evil spirits is high throughout Nigeria, this kind of public accusation can instill fear in people and cause them to mend their ways. Members of secret societies also can act as judges or intermediaries in disputes.

Military Activity. Nigeria's military consists of an army, a navy, an air force, and a police force. The minimum age for military service is eighteen.

The Nigerian military is the largest and best-equipped military in West Africa. As a member of the Economic Community of West African States (ECOWAS), Nigeria is the major contributor to the organization's military branch, known as ECOMOG. Nigerian troops made up the vast majority of the ECOMOG forces deployed to restore peace following civil wars in Liberia, Guinea-Bissau, and Sierra Leone. Public dissatisfaction with Nigeria's participation in the Sierra Leonean crisis was extremely high due to high casualty rates among the Nigerian soldiers. Nigeria pledged to pull out of Sierra Leone in 1999, prompting the United Nations to send in peacekeepers in an attempt stem the violence. While the foreign forces in Sierra Leone are now under the mandate of the United Nations, Nigerian troops still make up the majority of the peacekeepers.

Nigeria has a long-running border dispute with Cameroon over the mineral-rich Bakasi Peninsula, and the two nations have engaged in a series of cross-boarder skirmishes. Nigeria, Cameroon, Niger, and Chad also have a long-running border dispute over territory in the Lake Chad region, which also has led to some fighting across the borders.

Social Welfare and Change Programs

Severe poverty, human rights violations, and corruption are some of the major social ills that have plagued Nigeria for decades. Because Nigeria is in the midst of major political change, however, there is great hope for social reform in the country.

President Obasanjo's administration has been focusing much of its efforts on changing the world's image of Nigeria. Many foreign companies have been reluctant to invest in Nigeria for fear of political instability. Obasanjo hopes that if Nigeria can project the image of a stable nation, he can coax foreign investors to come to Nigeria and help bolster the country's failing economy. The World Bank and the International Monetary Fund (IMF) are also working with Nigeria to develop economic policies that will revitalize the nation's economy.

General Obasanjo also says that rooting out corruption in all levels of government is one of his top priorities.

A man sells patterned cloth at a market. Nigerians are expert dyers, weavers, and tailors.

He signed the Anti-Corruption Act in June 2000, creating a special commission for investigating charges of corruption brought by ordinary Nigerians against government officials.

According to Amnesty International's 2000 report, Nigeria's new government continues to make strides in improving human rights throughout the country, most notably in the release of political prisoners. However, the detention of journalists critical of the military and reports of police brutality continue to be problems. Foreign governments and watchdog organizations continue to press the Nigerian government for further human rights reforms.

Gender Roles and Statuses

Division of Labor by Gender. In general, labor is divided in Nigerian society along gender lines. Very few women are active in the political and professional arenas. In urban areas, increasing numbers of women are becoming involved in the professional workforce, but they are greatly outnumbered by their male counterparts. Women who do manage to gain professional employment rarely make it into the higher levels of management.

However, women in Nigeria still play significant roles in the economy, especially in rural areas. Women are often expected to earn significant portions of the family income. As a rule, men have little obligation to provide for their wives or children. Therefore women have traditionally had to farm or sell homemade products in the local market to ensure that they could feed and clothe their children. The division of labor along gender lines even exists within industries. For example, the kinds of crops that women cultivate differ from those that men cultivate. In Igbo society, yams are seen as men's crops, while beans and cassava are seen as women's crops.

The Relative Status of Women and Men. Modern Nigeria is a patriarchal society. Men are dominant over women in virtually all areas. While Nigeria is a signatory to the international Convention on Equality for Women, it means little to the average Nigerian woman. Women still have fewer legal rights than men. According to Nigeria's Penal Code, men have the right to beat their wives as long as they do not cause permanent physical injury. Wives are often seen as little more than possessions and are subject to the rule of their husbands.

However, women can exercise influence in some areas. For example, in most ethnic groups, mothers and sisters have great say in the lives of their sons and brothers, respectively. The blood relationship allows these women certain leeway and influence that a wife does not have.

Marriage, Family, and Kinship

Marriage. There are three types of marriage in Nigeria today: religious marriage, civil marriage, and traditional marriage. A Nigerian couple may decide to take part in one or all of these marriages. Religious marriages, usually Christian or Muslim, are conducted according to the norms of the respective religious teachings and take place in a church or a mosque. Christian males are allowed only one wife, while Muslim men can take up to four wives. Civil official weddings take place in a government registry office. Men are allowed only one wife under a civil wedding, regardless of religion. Traditional marriages usually are held at the wife's house and are performed according to the customs of the ethnic group involved. Most ethnic groups traditionally allow more than one wife.

Depending on whom you ask, polygamy has both advantages and disadvantages in Nigerian society. Some Nigerians see polygamy as a divisive force in the family, often pitting one wife against another. Others see polygamy as a unifying factor, creating a built-in support system that allows wives to work as a team.

While Western ways of courtship and marriage are not unheard of, the power of traditional values and the strong influence of the family mean that traditional ways are usually followed, even in the cities and among the elite. According to old customs, women did not have much choice of whom they married, though the numbers of arranged marriages are declining. It is also not uncommon for women to marry in their teens, often to a much older man. In instances where there are already one or more wives, it is the first wife's responsibility to look after the newest wife and help her integrate into the family.

Many Nigerian ethnic groups follow the practice of offering a bride price for an intended wife. Unlike a dowry, in which the woman would bring something of material value to the marriage, a bride price is some form of compensation the husband must pay before he can marry a wife. A bride price can take the form of money, cattle, wine, or other valuable goods paid to the woman's family, but it also can take a more subtle form. Men might contribute money to the education of an intended wife or help to establish her in a small-scale business or agricultural endeavor. This form of bride price is often incorporated as part of the wooing process. While women who leave their husbands will be welcomed back into their families, they often need a justification for breaking the marriage. If the husband is seen as having treated his wife well, he can expect to have the bride price repaid.

Though customs vary from group to group, traditional weddings are often full of dancing and lively music. There is also lots of excitement and cultural displays. For example, the Yoruba have a practice in which the bride and two or three other women come out covered from head to toe in a white shroud. It is the groom's job to identify his wife from among the shrouded women to show how well he knows his wife.

Divorce is quite common in Nigeria. Marriage is more of a social contract made to ensure the continuation of family lines rather than a union based on love and emotional connections. It is not uncommon for a husband and wife to live in separate homes and to be extremely independent of one another. In most ethnic groups, either the man or the woman can end the marriage. If the woman leaves her husband, she will often be taken as a second or third wife of another man. If this is the case, the new husband is responsible for repaying the bride price to the former husband. Children of a divorced woman are normally accepted into the new family as well, without any problems.

Domestic Unit. The majority of Nigerian families are very large by Western standards. Many Nigerian men take more than one wife. In some ethnic groups, the greater the number of children, the greater a man's standing in the eyes of his peers. Family units of ten or more are not uncommon.

In a polygamous family, each wife is responsible for feeding and caring for her own children, though the wives often help each other when needed. The wives also will take turns feeding their husband so that the cost of his food is spread equally between or among the wives. Husbands are the authority figures in the household, and many are not used to their ideas or wishes being challenged.

In most Nigerian cultures, the father has his crops to tend to, while his wives will have their own jobs, whether they be tending the family garden, processing palm oil, or selling vegetables in the local market. Children may attend school. When they return home, the older boys will help their father with his work, while the girls and younger boys will go to their mothers.

Inheritance. For many Nigerian ethnic groups, such as the Hausa and the Igbo, inheritance is basically a male affair. Though women have a legal right to inheritance in Nigeria, they often receive nothing. This is a reflection of the forced economic independence many women live under. While their husbands are alive, wives are often responsible for providing for themselves and their children. Little changes economically after the death of the husband. Property and wealth are usually passed on to sons, if they are old enough, or to other male relatives, such as brothers or uncles.

For the Fulani, if a man dies, his brother inherits his property and his wife. The wife usually returns to live with her family, but she may move in with her husband's brother and become his wife.

Kin Groups. While men dominate Igbo society, women play an important role in kinship. All Igbos, men and women, have close ties to their mother's clan, which usually lives in a different village. When an Igbo dies, the body is usually sent back to his mother's village to be buried with his mother's kin. If an Igbo is disgraced or cast out of his community, his mother's kin will often take him in.

For the Hausa, however, there is not much of a sense of wide-ranging kinship. Hausa society is based on the nuclear family. There is a sense of a larger extended family, including married siblings and their families, but there is little kinship beyond that. However, the idea of blood being thicker than water is very strong in Hausa society. For this reason, many Hausas will try to stretch familial relationships to the broader idea of clan or tribe to diffuse tensions between or among neighbors.

Socialization

Infant Care. Newborns in Nigerian societies are regarded with pride. They represent a community's and a family's future and often are the main reason for many marriages.

Throughout Nigeria, the bond between mother and child is very strong. During the first few years of a child's life, the mother is never far away. Nigerian women place great importance on breast-feeding and the bond that it creates between mother and child. Children are often not weaned off their mother's milk until they are toddlers.

Children who are too young to walk or get around on their own are carried on their mother's backs, secured by a broad cloth that is tied around the baby and fastened at the mother's breasts. Women will often carry their children on their backs while they perform their daily chores or work in the fields.

Child Rearing and Education. When children reach the age of about four or five, they often are expected to start performing a share of the household duties. As the children get older, their responsibilities grow. Young men are expected to help their fathers in the fields or tend the livestock. Young women help with the cooking, fetch water, or do laundry. These tasks help the children learn how to become productive members of their family and community. As children, many Nigerians learn that laziness is not acceptable; everyone is expected to contribute.

While children in most Nigerian societies have responsibilities, they also are allowed enough leeway to be children. Youngsters playing with homemade wooden dolls and trucks, or groups of boys playing soccer are common sights in any Nigerian village.

In many Nigerian ethnic groups, the education of children is a community responsibility. For example,

Nigerian people at a market.
Food plays a central role in the rituals of all ethnic groups in Nigeria.

in the Igbo culture the training of children is the work of both men and women, within the family and outside it. Neighbors often look after youngsters while parents may be busy with other chores. It is not strange to see a man disciplining a child who is not his own.

All Nigerian children are supposed to have access to a local elementary school. While the government aims to provide universal education for both boys and girls, the number of girls in class is usually much lower than the number of boys. Sending every child in a family to school can often put a lot of strain on a family. The family will lose the child's help around the house during school hours and will have to pay for uniforms and supplies. If parents are forced to send one child to school over another, many will choose to educate boys before girls.

Higher Education. Historically, Nigerians have been very interested in higher education. The lack of universities providing quality education equal to that in Britain was a major component of the social reforms that led to Nigeria's independence. Today there are forty-three universities in Nigeria. The majority of these are government-run, but the government has recently approved the creation of three private universities.

While Nigeria's system of higher education is the largest in Africa, the demand for higher education far exceeds the capacity of the facilities. There simply are not enough institutions to accommodate the demand. In 1998 only thirty-five thousand students were accepted to Nigerian universities out of a pool of more than four hundred thousand applicants.

Nigeria also has 125 technical training schools. The majority of these focus on polytechnic and agricultural training, with a few specializing in areas such as petroleum sciences and health.

Etiquette

Age is greatly respected in Nigeria. In an area where the average life expectancy is not very high, those who live into their senior years are seen as having earned special rights of respect and admiration. This is true of both men and women.

Socially, greetings are of the utmost importance. A handshake and a long list of well wishes for a counterpart's family and good health are expected when meeting someone. This is often true even if you have seen that person a short time earlier. Whether you are talking to a bank teller or visiting a friend, it is considered rude not to engage in a proper greeting before getting down to business.

Shaking hands, eating, or passing things with the left hand are unacceptable. The left hand is reserved for personal toiletries and is considered dirty.

Religion

Religious Beliefs. It is estimated that 50 percent of Nigerians are Muslim, 40 percent are Christian, and that the remaining 10 percent practice various indigenous religions.

While Muslims can be found in all parts of Nigeria, their strongest footholds are among the Hausa and the Yoruba. Islam in Nigeria is similar to Islam throughout the world. It is based on the teachings of the Prophet Muhammad, which are outlined in the Qur'an.

Christianity is most prevalent in the south of Nigeria. The vast majority of Igbo are Christians, as are many Yorubas. The most popular forms of Christianity in Nigeria include Anglican, Presbyterian, American Southern Baptist, and Methodist. Also, there are large pockets of Seventh-Day Adventists and Jehovah's Witnesses.

Conflict with the way some missionaries administered the churches during colonial times also created several breakaway African-Christian churches. Most of these adhere to the doctrines of Western churches but have introduced African music and tradition to their Masses. Some have even eased Christian restrictions on polygamy.

Relations between Christians and Muslims are tense in many areas. Since late 1999, numerous clashes between the two have led to thousands of deaths. The northern city of Kaduna has been the flash point for many of these riots, as local leaders discussed whether to institute Shari'a law in the region. Demonstrations by Christians against the idea soon led to violent confrontations with Muslims. The debate over Shari'a law and the violence accompanying it continue in many of the northern states.

While Islam and Christianity are the dominant religions in Nigeria, neither is completely free of influence from indigenous religions. Most people who consider themselves good Muslims or good Christians often also follow local religious practices. This makes up for perceived shortcomings in their religion. Most indigenous religions are based on a form of ancestor worship in which family members who have passed into the spirit world can influence things in the world of the living. This mixing of traditional ways with Islam has led to groups such as the Bori cult, who use spirit possession as a way to understand why people are suffering in this life. The mixing of traditional ways with Christianity has led to the development of the Aladura Church. Aladura priests follow basic Christian doctrine but also use prophecy, healing, and charms to ward off witchcraft.

Many Nigerians follow the teachings of purely indigenous religions. Most of these religions share the idea that one supreme god created the earth and its people, but has left people to decide their own paths in life. Followers of the traditional Yoruban religion believe that hundreds of spirits or minor gods have taken the place of the supreme god in influencing the daily lives of individuals. Many Yoruban slaves who were taken to the Caribbean and the Americas brought this religion with them. There it was used as the basis of Santeria and voodoo.

Because the vast majority of Igbos converted to Christianity during colonialism, few practice the traditional Igbo religion, which is based on hundreds of gods, not a single creator.

A man sits in front of his farmhouse in Toro, Nigeria. Traditionally, only men own land.

Religious Practitioners. According to Muslim and Christian traditions, officials in these religions tend to be male. For most indigenous religions, priests and priestesses are common. Traditional priests and priestesses get their power and influence from their ability to be possessed by their god or by their ability to tell the future or to heal. In the Igbo religion men serve as priests to Igbo goddesses, and women serve as priestesses to Igbo gods. While both men and women can rank high in the Yoruban religion, women usually are among the most respected of traditional priests.

Rituals and Holy Places. Because many of the indigenous religions are based on various spirits or minor gods, each with influence over a specific area of nature, many of the traditional rituals are based on paying homage to these gods and spirits. Likewise, the area of control for a spirit also marks the places that are holy to that spirit. For example, a tribe's water spirit may have a specific pond or river designated as its holy place. The Kalabari, Okrika, and Ikwerre tribes of the Niger Delta region all have festivals in honor of water spirits sacred to their peoples. The Yoruba hold a twenty-day <u>Shango</u> festival each year to honor their god of thunder. Many Igbo consider it bad luck to eat yams from the new harvest until after the annual Yam Festival, a harvest celebration held in honor of the Igbo earth goddess Ani.

Death and the Afterlife. Christian and Muslim Nigerians believe that following death, a person's soul is released and judged by God before hopefully going on to Heaven. Many traditional religions, especially those of the eastern tribes, believe in reincarnation. In these tribes, people believe that the dead will come back as a member of his or her mother's or sister's family. Many in-depth ceremonies are necessary to prepare the body before burial. For example, if the person was inflicted with some physical disability, steps would be taken to prevent it from being passed on to him in the next life. An infertile woman may have her abdomen cut open before burial or a blind man may have a salve made from special leaves placed over his eyes.

Regardless of religion, Nigerians bury their dead. This is customary among Christians and Muslims, but it also is based on traditional beliefs that the body should be returned to the earth that sustained it during life.

Muslims are buried so that their heads face the holy city of Mecca in Saudi Arabia. For others, it is customary to bury a man with his head turned toward the east, so he can see the rising sun. A woman is buried facing west, so she will know when the sun sets and when it is time to prepare dinner for her husband in the next life. People also cover the body with black earth during burial because many believe that red earth will result in skin blemishes in the next life.

The ethnic groups in eastern Nigeria believe that the more music and dancing at a funeral, the better that person's chances of a successful afterlife. The size of funerals depends on the social standing of the deceased. Men are expected to set aside money that will be used to ensure they have a properly elaborate funeral. Women, children, and adolescents tend to have much less elaborated funerals.

Medicine and Health Care

Neglect has left many clinics and hospitals in poor physical condition and without modern equipment. Pharmacies, both state-run and private, regularly run out of medicines. Patients looking for cheaper remedies often turn to black-market vendors, who often sell expired or counterfeit drugs. There also is a shortage of qualified medical personnel to adequately treat the whole population.

In 2000, the estimated life expectancy of Nigerian men and women was fifty-one years. The estimated infant mortality rate was over 7 percent, or about seventy-four infant deaths for every thousand live births.

Both Western and traditional forms of medicine are popular in Nigeria. Traditional medicine, also known as *juju,* is common at the rural level. Practitioners of juju use a variety of plants and herbs in their cures. Most families also have their own secret remedies for minor health problems.

Many rural people do not trust Western-style medicine, preferring instead to use traditional ways. In many instances the traditional medicine is very effective and produces fewer side effects than modern drugs. Most of modern medicine's prescription drugs grew out of traditional herbal remedies. However, there are conditions in which traditional medicine can do more harm than good. Sometimes this leads to conflict between the government-sponsored health care system and traditional ways. Some organizations are now looking at ways to combine the two in an attempt to coax people back into health centers.

The federal government is responsible for the training of health care workers and running nationwide health campaigns such as those aimed at fighting AIDS, Guinea worm infection, river blindness, and leprosy.

Secular Celebrations

Nigeria observes three secular national holidays and several officially recognized Muslim and Christian holidays when government, commerce, and banks are closed. The secular holidays are New Year's Day (1 January), Workers' Day (1 May), and National Day (1 October). The Christian holidays are Christmas (25 December), Good Friday, and Easter Monday. The Muslim holidays are Eid al-Fitr (the last day of Ramadan, the Muslim holy month of fasting), Tabaski, and Eid al-Moulid. Aside from Christmas, the religious holidays fall on different days each year.

The Arts and Humanities

Support for the Arts. Nigerian art traditionally served a social or religious purpose and did not exist for the sake of art per se. For example, dance was used to teach or to fulfill some ritualistic goal. Sculpture was used in blessings, in healing rituals, or to ward off bad luck. With increasing modernization, however, Nigerian art is becoming less oriented to a particular purpose. In some cases, Nigerians have abandoned whole forms of art because they no longer served a purpose. For example, the elaborate tombstones once widely produced by the Ibibio are becoming increasingly rare as Western-style cemeteries are replacing traditional burial grounds.

The government has recognized this decline in Nigerian art. In an attempt to promote Nigerian nationalism through art, it has launched some programs, such as

Women engrave designs into yellow calabash gourds. Nigerian art traditionally served a social or religious purpose.

the All-Nigeria Festival of Arts, to revitalize the Nigerian art world. Many wealthy Nigerians looking to recapture their roots, as well as Western tourists and collectors looking for an African art experience, are willing to spend money on Nigerian art. This has led to a slight revival of the art industry.

Literature. Nigeria has a long and incredibly rich literary history. Nigerians are traditionally storytellers. Much of pre-colonial history in Nigeria is the result of stories handed down from generation to generation. With colonization and the introduction of reading, writing, and the English language, Nigerian storytellers soon began sharing their talents with a worldwide audience. Perhaps Nigeria's most famous writer is Wole Soyinka, who won the 1986 Nobel Prize for literature. His most famous works include *A Dance of the Forests, The Swamp Dwellers,* and *The Lion and the Jewel.* Other famous Nigerian authors include Chinua Achebe, whose *Things Fall Apart* is a favorite among Western schools as an example of the problems inflicted on African societies during colonization, and Ben Okri, whose novel *The Famished Road* won Britain's 1991 Booker Prize.

Graphic Arts. Nigeria is famous for its sculpture. The bronze work of the ancient cities of Ife and Benin can be found in museums all over the world. These areas in southern Nigeria still produce large amounts of bronze castings. Woodcarvings and terra-cotta sculptures also are popular.

Nigerians are expert dyers, weavers, and tailors. They produce massive quantities of beautiful, rich, and colorful textiles. However, the majority of these are sold primarily for everyday wear and not as examples of art.

Performance Arts. Dance and music are perhaps the two most vibrant forms of Nigerian art. Nigerian music is dependent on strong rhythms supplied by countless drums and percussion instruments. Highlife is a type of music heavily influenced by Western culture. It sounds like an Africanized version of American big band or ballroom music. Afro-beat combines African rhythms and melodies with jazz and soul.

CREATION OF PIDGIN LANGUAGE AND ITS USAGE IN NIGERIA.

So much has been discussed, in the literature, of the emergence of pidgins around the world as a language of contact. Pidgin has since developed from a *makeshift* language into a fully crystallized and expanded language today. It has transited, over the decades from a minimal pidgin through a stabilized pidgin onto an expanded pidgin and now, in parts of the Niger Delta in Nigeria, involving people of dissimilar cultural linguistic backgrounds, to becoming a Creole.

The aim of this topic is to describe the burgeoning sociolinguistic situation of the Pidgin language, as we attempt to pigeon-hole the inherent semantic and pragmatic usage of the language, arising from substrate influences which derive from the various Nigerian local language cultures. It speaks volumes of a ready acceptance of the new form of Pidgin which signals a readiness for national integration in Nigeria despite obvious socio-cultural and linguistic differences among its speakers countrywide.

Origins and development of Pidgin

The English based pidgin which is spoken in Nigeria was cultured in the Niger Delta region of the country. Many critics of the language argue that pidgin originated as a result of contact between European traders who came, sailing along the West African coast and met the peoples in the region of the lower Niger tributaries. Evidence abounds of materials found in original manuscript sources of trade voyages between Europe and Africa, from the fifteenth to nineteenth

century, which lie presently in archives and in printed sources in London, Paris, Rome, Lisbon and The Hague. This body of evidence, in their ontological state, attests to the fact of Pidgin use in the extant but moribund Benin kingdom of Nigeria and along the trading coast of West Africa up to the Bight of Benin, and a little way hinterland. Until recent as the 1980s when Pidgin began to gain greater significance all around the Nigerian country, it had remained basically a trade language among communities or among people who do not speak each other's language. This is besides the old thinking that Pidgin was the language used by people of little or no education and generally, the language of those with lower social economic status. And this gave it the semblance of a stigmatized language. For this reason, the Pidgin language was repudiated by the educated elite in Nigeria for so long. And for that length of time, linguists in Nigeria did pay little or no attention to Pidgin, which was why it lacked, until latterly, a standard (written) model because it is learned informally.

By this very fact, Pidgin had no fixed convention of orthography; no standardization, until the naissance of the Naija Languej Akẹdẹmi (NLA), a school which seeks to develop and to defend the Pidgin language in Nigeria.

Indeed, Pidgin became stabilized somewhat when it began to acquire certain norms of meaning, pronunciation and grammar with variation, though, resulting from the transfer of features from speakers' first languages. Arising from the twin factor of time and broadening of contact between the peoples of Nigeria and migrants into the country, the Nigeria Pidgin gained a forward leap in its development and growth to assume an extended proportion of use especially in the Southern parts of the country.

The diversity of linguistic groups in Nigeria, it must be stated, tended to create some medley in the Pidgin (lexico-semantic and pragmatic) usage amongst the older generation of users of the language in the country. But such diversity of usage, today, in some sense, enriches, to a large extent, the lexicon of the language which is enhanced by the many new words and expressions from the majority and minority languages, as could be used in combination even in a single sentence by the younger generation of speakers of the new wave Pidgin language. And because the language is fast spreading in the multicultural and multilingual society of Nigeria at large, different dialects of the language abound with as many local varieties or sociolects as there are major speech communities that have adopted the use of the language, ranging from one geographical location to another. It follows, therefore, that Pidgin in Nigeria is heavily influenced by substrate languages in lexis, phonology, syntax and semantics although, essentially, it is English lexified; the main language from which it derives its superstrate influence. Thus, the lexical, phonological, syntactic and semantic meanings that derive from the Nigeria Pidgin rely heavily on the languages and cultures of the host regions or communities where it is spoken. See, for instance, the expression: **Ọdiọ nna di rat we de put hol fọ pọt**. This means "Ọdiọn is the rat that drills a hole into a cooking pot". Semantically, this statement presupposes that "Ọdiọn is a traitor or a sell-out". Again, we have: **Ọmọnigho teks hem chọp winch**. This expression denotes that

Ọmọnigho ingested witchcraft willy-nilly [for being too shy to turn down the offer in order not to offend the giver]. The semantic connotation here is that

Ọmọnigho agreed to terms and conditions that were not agreeable with her, or that she acquiesced regardless. In this respect, the Nigeria Pidgin has become, for most of its users, a language of cognition.

Pidgin in Nigeria, initially had no native speakers, but at the moment, the language finds *nativity*, as it were, amongst its present-day users whose various regional language backgrounds serve the cultural inputs which, to a large extent, influence the positive development of the language in our day. Thus the Nigeria Pidgin could be said to be transiting through a like-process of nativization via influences of language cultures. Cultural influence, therefore, is part of the development of the Nigeria Pidgin which involves introducing into the language new concepts, values and modes of interactions as a reflection of the Nigerian regional language cultures. Ayo Bamgbose (1995)says this could be matched by the adoption of certain ways of life which relate to modes of dressing, food, religion, trees, musical instruments, titles, etc. The result is a transfer of patterns from the first or regional language of the speaker into phonological, lexical, semantic and syntactic patterns of the second language as with the Nigeria Pidgin nowadays. Furthermore, Bamgbose speaks of the new *form* "not [only] limited to the usual features of transfer of phonological, lexical, syntactic and semantic patterns ... [but] also concerned with the creative development of ... [a language] including the evolution of distinctively Nigerian usage, attitudes and pragmatic use of the language"(21). He identified three aspects of the process of development viz: the linguistic, the pragmatic and the creative development which Iyang Udofot(2003) re-branded the linguistic, the lexico-semantic and the morpho-semantic features respectively.

Linguistic features of Nigeria Pidgin

The English related pidgins in use, according to George Yule (2000), "are characterized by an absence of any complex grammatical morphology and a limited vocabulary" (234). Southerland and Katamba (1996) observe that pidgins "usually present a syntactic structure that is comparatively simple and they exhibit certain characteristic relationships to their source languages. They normally reflect the influence of their higher status (or dominant) languages in their lexicon and that of the lower status language in their phonology (and occasionally syntax)"(572). Strictly speaking, this is what the Nigeria Pidgin represents. It must be stated clearly here that besides the ancestor language influences on the West African pidgins, English supplied more of the vocabulary to Nigeria Pidgin while the Nigerian local languages have more influence on the grammar of the language which tend to have a simplified structure in its morphology, phonology and syntax. It is unlike the English system which has inflections for gender, number and person on the noun and tense, and verb negation, et cetera. Users of the Nigeria Pidgin often express themselves in words and sentences that have certain peculiarities of grammar and meanings which bear carry-over effects from their cultural ways of speaking onto Pidgin. Such ways are now being adopted by other speakers from the other regions of the country, in addition to their own modes of speech –all to complement the new form of Pidgin usage. Consequently, anew mode of the Nigeria Pidgin speech is gradually emerging among its speakers in general with some features that remain peculiar to the language overall, seen in the following sub-headings.

3.1 Phonological features

Phonologically, the sound system of the Nigeria Pidgin is simple, having almost entirely eliminated the elaborate morphology of English. A general trend in the segmental and non segmental features and in the functions of the Nigeria Pidgin can be discerned as follows:

3.1.1 Segmental features

The Nigeria Pidgin, far more than the English language, uses fewer of segmental features which show tendencies of approximation in the Pidgin from English language pronunciations as in the following:

Consonants

The Nigeria Pidgin speech is involved in the substitution of the symbols of first consonants of the speaker's or regional language to replace, for example, the voiced and voiceless dental fricatives /ð/ and /Ө/ with the voiced and voiceless alveolar plosives /t/ and /d/ as in **dat** for *that* and **tin** for *thing*. This pattern is also repeated with the velar nasal /ŋ/ sound which is replaced by the alveolar nasal /n/ sound as in /nɔӨŋ/, a word which, in itself, is pronounced [**nọtin**] among speakers of Pidgin in Nigeria. The voiced and voiceless post-alveolar affricate sound /ʧ/ and /ʤ/are replaced by the voiced and voiceless post-alveolar fricative sounds /ʃ/ and /ʒ/, as in the pronunciation of "**church**" /ʧə:ʧ/ which in Nigeria Pidgin is often pronounced "**chọch**" [ʃɔʃ].

This is also true of "**judge**" /ʤʌʤ/ which is pronounced "**jọj**" /ʒɔʒ/, etc. Generally speaking, there is a transfer in the use of diagraphs, of the "labial-velar" plosives /kp/ as in "**kpẹlẹ**", as well as in the bilabial plosive and velar affricate sounds /gb/ and /gh/ respectively, both in the example word "**gbeghe**", etc. from the stock of consonant sounds of the Nigerian speakers' first languages into Pidgin. This also applies to the nasal sound /ɲ/, which is realized in the palate-alveolar region in the words "**nyanga**" and "**nyanfunnyanfun**", etc.

Strictly speaking, this sound is different from the English alveolar nasal sound /ŋ/ which is equally functional in Nigeria Pidgin. Another innovation in the example of a consonant used in the local language dominated.

Minimally, the Nigeria Pidgin vowels can co-occur freely to form a set of diphthongs in the language such as the **[ọi]**, **[au]** and **[ai]** sound sequence in **bọi**(boy), **shaut**(shout) and **mai**(my) respectively. Through the Nigeria Pidgin vowel sounds, speakers of the language around the country maximally realize the Monophthongisation of diphthongs and triphthongs. However, the Nigeria Pidgin

neither uses the basic English diphthongs [the /əu/, /uə/ and /ei/] and

triphthong[the /aiə / and /auə/] sounds as a result of its different system. For this reason, a diphthong in English, say, in the word "take" /teik/ will be

pronounced **[tek]** in Nigeria Pidgin, and an English triphthong as "tyre" /taiə/ will be **[taya]**, etc.

3.1.2 Non-segmental features

Strictly speaking, the Nigeria Pidgin is a tone language, like most African languages, with high and low distinctions. It is at the same time syllable-timed. Indeed, Mafeni, like Oyebade above, have shown that tones are used in Nigeria Pidgin to distinguish between the lexical and grammatical meanings in a significant number of minimal pairs. In addition to this, the South Western variety spoken in Warri, Sapele and Uvwie has some distinctive intonation with varied speakers, some of whom use the language as mother tongue. Thus, Oyebade argues that the Nigeria Pidgin is a "pitch accent language" where "both the tonal and the intonational pitch systems have become … intertwined" (71).

Besides other characteristics, we notice the relocation of stress on syllables by accent in the production of sounds in Nigeria Pidgin words like **[prọˈpa]**, the equivalence of the English word "proper" which a speaker of English would preferably pronounce [ˈprɔpə]; **[bẹˈta]**, the equivalence of "better"

which the same speaker of English would preferably pronounce [ˈbetə]. This much goes for the pidgin word **[gadˈrum]**, the equivalence of "guardroom" which pronunciation in English is [ˈgaːdruëm], etc.

3.2 Lexical features

Because the Nigeria Pidgin is English-related, most of its vocabulary, and by extension, its word pronunciations tend to sound like English, its *higher* lexifier language.

By this very fact, the outlying influence of the Nigeria Pidgin is, indeed, English while the language has, as its substratum and underlying influence, the Nigerian local languages. Without a doubt, much of its earlier vocabulary derives from the remnants of the ancestor languages of the nucleus pidgin –Portuguese, Dutch, and actually, a few from Spanish and French, most of which were handed down to the English in their first and second comings for trading and missionary purposes (see *Benin and the Europeans 1485 to 1897*, 1977). And such words, from the aforementioned Western European languages of higher status influence on West African pidgins became relexified and sometime, had their meanings extended to produce **pikin**=(Portuguese, *pequeno*)=small one/child/infant, **hala**=(French, *holloer*)=holler/yell/shout, **sabi**=(Portuguese, *saber;* Spanish, *sabe*)=savvy/know/practical knowledge, **alele**=(French, *aller*)=go/move

vẹks=(French,vexer)=vex/angry,palava=(Portuguese, palavra)=speech/trouble/dilemma,

bọku=(French, *beaucoup*)=many/plentiful/abundance, etc. These, and many more, have been retained in the present-day Nigeria Pidgin lexicon and usage. Added to this is the loan translation/creation from the Nigerian indigenous languages which beef up the vocabulary of the language to give it new domains of use. Besides the earlier examples provided in section two of local word inputs, such loan creation from the Nigerian indigenous languages, which have not by themselves experienced morphological changes nor relexification like their Western European language counterpart examples above, includes local words, adopted and now used by the generality of speakers; words like :

yanga=(Hausa)=pride/vanity,**wọwọ**=(Edo/Delta)=ugly/unattractive, **ọga**=(Yoruba)=boss/master, **isi-ewu**=(Igbo)=goat-headdelicacy, **agbero**=(Yoruba)=motor-park tout/uncouth, **wayo**=(Hausa)=trick/deceit/sophistry, **una** from the word *unu*]=(Igbo)=[plural form of] you, **shakara**=(Yoruba)=show-off/bravado/, **tatafo**=(Edo/Delta)=gossip/tell-tale, **jọọ**=(Yoruba)=I beg of you/please, etc. all serving to enrich the lexicon of the Nigeria Pidgin. Again, we have examples of words belonging to everyday register of food, dress, insult, interjections, titles, etc. as loan words into the Nigeria Pidgin, emanating from different Nigerian language cultures.

Certainly, the Pidgin language, like many languages in the world, at the moment, is a mixture composed of elements from foreign and many Nigerian local sources. This gives the language a unique character because going by the current tradition of lexicon expansion, the Nigeria Pidgin ceases to be a product of one clear historical evolution.

3.2.1 Lexico-semantic features

Undeniably, speakers of the Nigeria Pidgin device certain linguistic means to extend their vocabulary via lexico-semantic and pragmatic features arising from mother tongue influence which is transferred into Pidgin. Through the processes of multifunctionality, polysemy and circumlocution, the lexicon of Nigeria Pidgin have been influenced by European and African lexical sources including morphological and semantic changes in the processes of lexical loaning/retention, coining, semantic shifts, reduplication and calquing. This, according to

Nicholas Faraclas (1996) includes, among others, compounding, prepositions, serialized verb constructions, ideophones, etc. Again, expressions that bear the semantic extension of meanings can also be found in Nigeria Pidgin usage most of which two base words or compound words are combined to form a coinage, or a new word with an extended meaning derived, such as:

- **tai-fes–** to bear creased brows when upset • **waka-jugbe–** to roam aimlessly

- **skata laf–** to break into sudden laughter
- **pik res –** to break into a sudden race
- **swit-maut–** the art of sophistry • **bad-maut–** the art of sarcasm, et cetera.

3.3 Morpho-semantic features

The Creative development or morpho-semantic expressions are found in the direct transfer of Nigerian local expressions into the Pidgin, or expressions created into the language through morphological processes, having unique and clear-cut semantic implications from their traditional meanings. Certainly, there is a morphological process of a free morpheme or the base form of a (single) word that can stand on its own but which combines with another free morpheme to become two compound morphemes. Such two morphemes often come together to present a new coinage of a unique meaning, seen in some of the examples above such as: **swit +maut = swit-maut, pik + res = pik-res, skata + laf = skata-laf, tai + fes = tai-fes, bad + maut = bad-maut,** etc. Yet, Janet Holmes adds: "words generally do not have inflections, as in English, to mark the plural or to signal the tense of the verb" (91). Like most pidgins, therefore, the archetypal and correct Nigeria Pidgin expressions contain structures which lack inflectional suffixes on nouns, such that the possessive 's as well as the plural -s are not to be included in the structures, **di man haus**(i.e., **The man house**) to mean **the man's house** and **tri hankachif**(i.e., **Three handkerchief**) to mean **three handkerchiefs** respectively. And, finding a commonality with the pidgin of its origins, the Nigeria Pidgin system of modal expressions, in their roots and inflected forms – shall/should, can/could, will/would, may/might – have but one simplified system of marking tense in the present continuous form:

[fit …] or [go fit …]; (this latter form, obtained in some basilectal usages) to express possibility or necessity, is used as a paradigm for all of the modals. Further examples of creative/morpho-semantic expressions in Nigeria Pidgin usage will be found in the following expressions:

1. **A bẹg, anọ fit dai.** (Oh no! I cannot work myself to death/bring myself to ruin)
2. **Odjugo dọn opun ai tiyẹ.** (Odjugo now has a sense of wisdom)
3. **Hm-m, yu dọn hama!** (Surely, you have hit a jackpot!)
4. **God dọn bọta mai brẹd.** (Now, my prayers are answered)
5. **A bẹg, mek yu nọ puọ san san fọ mai garri.** (Please don't [pour sand into my meal of garri] ruin my chances)

Much of creative development also occurs in Pidgin literary writings where idioms, witty remarks and figurative expressions are translated from a speaker's cultural language into the Nigeria Pidgin to reflect the character of the language.

3.4 Syntactic features

The Nigeria Pidgin has a Subject/Verb/Object (SVO) sentence structure. It shares same characteristics with other pidgins: "word order is fixed; there is little or no inflection; negation usually involves a "no" word in front of the verb; nouns and verbs are regular; the … vocabulary is used creatively; and speakers use local idioms, metaphors, and proverbs" (*Encarta Dictionaries*, 2008). As noted by Elugbe and Omamor, the speech or vocabulary of the pidgin spoken in the Niger-Delta sounds like English though, but "not so the structure that emerged when Nigerians tried to string these words together" (9).

Essentially outstanding are two or one other characteristic, which are exceptional in the sense that they follow the pattern of structures from most Nigerian local languages. Such features include:
The omission of articles before titles and proper nouns in a sentence like **"If [ ] C.M.A. se dat adu sọmtin, mek a se anọ du am?"** (*Skeleton*, 61), **"[ ] Dẹvu bẹn yọ nẹk"]** (*Skeleton, 69*) **and "ivun [ ] gọvmẹnt nọ de laik am"** (*Skeleton, 70*), etc.

On the other hand, we notice with most speakers the inclusion of the morpheme **–o** as a topicalizer, which helps to avoid positing a phantom verb "be" in the following words/expressions: "… tafficator-o [**tafiketọ-o**], mirror-o [**mirọ-o**], bumber-o [**bọmba –o**], …"(*Skeleton, 63*). It is common knowledge that within the discourse-related properties of the internal information structure of topic and focus of a language, the lexical domain noun phrase in structures likes "be it the traffic indicator", "(be it) the mirror" or "(be it) (even) the bumper" is assumed to be the structural layer at which predicate-argument relations are defined (see Enoch Aboh, 2004). But far more than English does, the Nigeria Pidgin optimizes on the exchange of information between speaker and hearer.

3.5 Pragmatic features

Some of the instances of the manner in which Nigerian cultures have impinged on local pidgin usage bear testimony on the rule of language use typical of the Nigeria Pidgin in native situations. Bamgbose notes that the pattern of indigenous greetings is reflected in the use of such expression as *sorry* (expression of sympathy e.g. to a person who bashes a foot accidentally against a stone, or to someone who had just had a misfortune), *well-done* (greeting to anyone at work), *thanks for yesterday* (appreciation for favor done the previous day), *till tomorrow* (a greeting which may stand for "good night"), et cetera which definitely have found their way into Nigeria Pidgin from Nigeria English usage (a super stratum influence to the former). Other examples are found in:

Politeness and respect,
Solidarity, Greetings, etc.

The Role of Language in Literacy

Although definitions of literacy have broadened over the years to include a wide range of skills, the basic skills of reading and writing remain at the core of any definition of literacy, while numeracy skills are viewed as supplementary. Also, these definitions do not specify language of literacy, thereby leaving the decision to individual countries. UNESCO's (EFA, 2005) long-standing definition of basic literacy does not specify the language of literacy: ―A literate person is one who can, with understanding, both read and write a short simple statement on his or her everyday life‖ (p.153).

Neither is the language of literacy specified in UNESCO's definition of functional literacy:

A person is functionally literate who can engage in all those activities in which literacy is required for effective functioning of his (or her) group and community and also for enabling him (or her) to continue to use reading, writing and calculation for his (or her) own and the community's development. (p.30)

Indeed, there is evidence to support expanded definitions that take into account continuous acquisition of new skills such as those brought about by the technological age. There is some evidence that points to a growing number of educated but functional illiterates who are unable to perform certain daily tasks that characterise the current information technology age such as the ability to use the basic functions of a mobile phone (Ofulue, 2008). McCaffery et al. (2007) offer a layered view of literacy comprising skills, tasks, practices, and critical reflection, and emphasis could be on any layer depending on the purpose:

Literacy is rooted in the skills of reading and writing. These skills are used by individuals to accomplish tasks in their daily lives. These tasks are part of their literacy practices, socially and culturally rooted in the communities in which they live and work. Literacy can be a means for critical reflection on the world as a necessary part of becoming capable of creating change.

There are also country-based definitions of literacy, which, in general, reflect its core concept, that is the ability to read and write, but with some variations. These various definitions, which have implications for how literacy is measured, vary in their language considerations, for example ability to write with understanding 1) in any language, 2) in a specified language, and 3) in at least one language. However, the critical question remains, in which language is attainment of literacy being measured and, by implication, in which language(s) is literacy learned or practiced? Based on research, which has shown that acquiring literacy in one's mother tongue enhances access to literacy in other languages, UNESCO (2003) has consistently encouraged the use of the mother tongue in education. The reality, however, is that many children around the world begin their schooling using a second language (Ouane 2003, EFA 2010). And many others are excluded by virtue of the non-availability of literacy opportunities in their mother tongues. With greater attention being paid to the role of language in literacy, the issue of in which language literacy should be learned becomes a very important consideration. The issue is even more critical for multilingual contexts like Nigeria. The linguistically diverse nature of Nigeria's language terrain has made this question a difficult and complex one to answer over the years and even more so in the current dispensation where additional variables, such as the negative effect of the minority/major language dichotomy on minority languages, are observed.

Nigeria's Demographic, Language, and Literacy Profile

Nigeria is the most populous country in Africa and the ninth most populous country in the world with a linguistically diverse population of over 140 million people, about 510 spoken languages, and a literacy rate of 66% (UNICEF, 2009; Ethnologue, 2009). Population size is a key criterion for the classification of major versus minor languages. Approximately half of the population speak the three major languages, Hausa, Igbo, and Yoruba, as first or second languages. Regional languages are spoken by about one tenth of the population, namely Fulfulde, Nupe, Kanuri, Idoma, Tiv, Ibibio, Edo, Efik, and Ijaw, while the remaining languages are small group/minority languages. Many of these languages, especially the small group languages, have not been developed; they do not have orthographies and have not been assigned any significant role. Adegbija (2004) observed that only about 65 Nigerian languages have orthographies. English is Nigeria's official language and language of education; thus, it dominates the sociolinguistic space in terms of attitudes, power, and socioeconomic mobility. Going by Nigeria's literacy rate, about 66% of the population is literate in English, but there is no precise figure. The percentage given in this study is the percentage for the literate population in Nigeria as reported by UNICEF (2009), and it is based on school enrolment figures with English as the language of education. However, Adegbija (2003) was of the view that the population of English speakers is less than 20% of the population. Adegbija (1994) aptly surmises the linguistically diverse nature of

Nigeria's population when he notes that —although precise statistics are not available, one can safely conclude from the evidence available that no language in Nigeria is spoken by as many as 50% of the entire population as a first language (p.16).

Base d on Bamgbose's (1991) language topology, Nigeria shows the participation of at least five language types for literacy and communication and is illustrated in

Table 1

Language Typology

SN	Language type	Function	Languages involved
1	Mother tongue	Medium of informal education in the home and among peers within immediate community	All Nigerian languages
2	Language of immediate community	Local or regional lingua franca	All Nigerian languages, minority languages in particular
3	Language of wider communication	Wider reach for education, and communication as lingua franca, national language. Also, official language which is second language for most and first language for a growing number.	Official (English) national (Hausa, Igbo and Yoruba) and regional (Fulfulde, Nupe, Kanuri, Idoma, Tiv, Ibibio, Edo, Efik, and Ijaw).
4	Language of religion	Language of religious communication	Arabic
5	Language of wider communication	International communication	French

Source: Bamgbose (1991)

Research has shown that the most effective choice of language for basic literacy should be the language the child or adult is most familiar with (Adegbija, 2003). The language for conducting subsequent phases of literacy will depend on several factors, including the learner's profile (age, language needs, attitudes, and language skills already acquired) and the level/type of interaction with the immediate and wider society. These as well as other factors such as the historical experience, sociolinguistic features, and nationalistic views are considered in the choice of languages for education in Africa (Obanya, 2004, p.225). Nigeria's profile illustrates the complexities of language issues in multilingual nations as they seek ways to achieve mass literacy in learners' multiple languages.

Language Policy and Literacy

Language policies play a significant role in the spread of literacy. There is a strong link between language policies and the attitudes towards choice and development of indigenous languages. As noted in the EFA report (2005),

Language policies and practices have played, and continue to play, an important role in literacy and the development of literate communities. National language policies – the designation of an official language, the choice of language of instruction in schools and adult learning programmes – can facilitate or hinder language development and literacy acquisition. Research consistently shows that learning to read and write in one's mother tongue enhances access to literacy in other languages. Yet literacy efforts in many countries lack a clear language policy.

Nigeria's language policy is embedded within its education policy with the ultimate goal of promoting literacy in the English language while also achieving a degree of proficiency in a select number of Nigerian languages. The National Policy on Education (2004) states:

Government appreciates the importance of language as a means of promoting social interaction and natural cohesion; and preserving cultures. Thus every child shall learn the language of the immediate environment. Furthermore, in the interest of national unity it is expedient that every child shall be required to learn one of the three Nigerian languages: Hausa, Igbo and Yoruba. For smooth interaction with our neighbors, it is desirable for every Nigerian to speak French. Accordingly, French shall be the second official language in Nigeria and it shall be compulsory in primary and Junior Secondary Schools but a Non-Vocational Elective at the Senior Secondary School...The medium of instruction in the primary school shall be the language of the environment for the first three years. During this period, English shall be taught as a subject. From the fourth year, English shall progressively be used as a medium of instruction and the language of the immediate environment and French shall be taught as subjects.

In principle, Nigeria's language policy on education prescribes a role for all Nigerian languages that are languages of the immediate environment as languages of instruction for pre-primary and the first three of six years of primary education. English is prescribed as a medium of instruction from the fourth year of primary education onwards, and as a subject. A minimum of one national language is prescribed for learning as a subject at the secondary education level. French is a recent feature in the policy as a second official language and is prescribed for learning as a subject. In other words, the learner should be literate in a minimum of three to four languages at the end of 12 years of formal schooling. The policy is silent on the language of instruction for mass literacy, adult, and non-formal education. The assumption is that the language of instruction would be in the language of the immediate environment.

Language policies affect attitudes because prescription of which language should be used for what is a key factor that affects the attitudes of groups towards their mother tongues (Ouane, 2003). In countries like Nigeria where the policy assigns important roles to the exogenous language, that is English, it is only natural that attitudes towards learning using the mother tongue will suffer. By virtue of its accorded status, there is a greater motivation toward acquiring English via formal education than toward acquiring Nigerian languages. Although the policy prescribes a function for Nigerian languages, the cost of promoting learning in multiple languages is often cited as a major challenge to its implementation. The result is a migration to languages of instruction within the immediate environment for which materials are available. Urban/rural population statistics for Nigeria show that a greater percentage (52%) of the population lives in rural areas where the mother tongue is usually the first and sometimes only language spoken by pre-primary school learners. The language policy, as practiced, excludes a fair percentage of these learners from literacy because the language of instruction is not their mother tongue. In the urban setting, it is doubtful that the policy is being implemented as most schools use English as the preferred medium of instruction. Language policies should be designed to promote literacy in the mother tongues by assigning to them functionally significant roles that are equally as important as those assigned to the languages of power, which are used to attract positive economic and social benefits to the speakers and thus have a positive impact on learners' attitudes towards their mother tongue. Based on the Indian experience,

Rao (2007) observes that a clearly articulated framework for achieving literacy is a major factor in ensuring effective implementation of sound policies. Such a framework should adopt a multilingual approach for the training of teachers to teach in multiple languages and for the development of both teaching and supplementary reading materials in multiple languages.

Teacher Development

The EFA (2005) report notes the vital importance of teachers to the success of literacy programs, yet the lack of adequate and regular remuneration, job security, training opportunities, and continuous professional support have undermined their importance. The report also states that —unless the professional development of literacy educators and their trainers is taken seriously, progress towards more literate societies will be severely constrained‖ (p. 35). Teaching within multilingual contexts is often beset by problems of language materials, curriculum, time allocation, and availability of teachers (Bamgbose, 1991; Obanya, 2004). Instructional delivery is still very much dependent on traditional text methods in the absence of other forms of resources. Traditional methods require large numbers of teachers, infrastructure, and language materials.

(Bamgbose, 1991; Obanya, 2004). Instructional delivery is still very much dependent on traditional text methods in the absence of other forms of resources. Traditional methods require large numbers of teachers, infrastructure, and language materials. Although these issues are not unique to language teaching, coping with multiple languages that require a multiple number of teachers and materials becomes an issue. As is the case with highly populated countries burdened with high budget requirements for formal and informal education, the implementation of a language policy involving multiple languages for literacy becomes an additional burden. Although teacher development has improved over time, the EFA progress report notes that in many developing countries including Nigeria, there is still a shortfall in the number of trained teachers. To address the problem, a focus on teacher development was adopted as one of the resolutions at the 7th Ministers' Review Conference of E-9 countries. However, the training of teachers in the language(s) for literacy should perhaps be given more emphasis than it currently receives because the acquisition of language skills is the basis for literacy and subsequent skills for development.

Multilingualism and Language Development

In addressing issues of multilingualism in adult literacy, Robinson (2007) states:

Literacy is about communication and is therefore fundamentally a language-based activity; there can be no discussion of literacy without asking in which language literacy will be acquired and practiced and this implies a clear knowledge of what languages specific groups of people use for communication in their daily lives. There is a strong link between language and literacy especially in multilingual contexts where the language for formal education is often prescribed, while that of informal education is usually negotiated depending on the language of the immediate or wider community and on the availability of teaching resources in that language. The number of languages recommended by the policy implies that a learner will be exposed to at least four languages apart from the mother tongue over a period of 12 years of schooling. Indeed, linguistic diversity appears to be a crucial factor in accessing learning in correlation with high population, poverty, and literacy rates. According to the EFA (2006) report on literacy, a majority of countries facing salient literacy challenges are linguistically diverse. Decisions on language must balance political and ethnic sensitivity, pedagogical effectiveness, costs and learner preferences. The extra cost of training teachers and developing materials in multiple languages must be weighed against the inefficiency of teaching in languages that learners do not understand. A multilingual policy should also ensure that learners have opportunities to gain literacy skills in a second/official language that may be of wider use.

PRELIMENARY ATTITUDE OF ENGLISH LANGUAGE SPEAKERS AS SECOND LANGUAGE IN NIGERIA.

The early speakers of English Language used it to communicate among themselves that is to say among the diverse ethnic groups. They also used it to trade, especially in Lagos where many people had trooped in from the South, East, North and West of Nigeria. The language was spoken as pidgin until few who went to school started speaking Queen's English, which was Standard English.

Gradually, the language led people who became workers under the colonial master to embrace the English dressing, behaviour and negligence of their cultures.

This resulted in segregation and class identification of the elite and the illiterates.

The ruralists and the urbanists have nothing to do with education but reveal the new image of Nigerian dwellers in both. Thus rural dwellers trooped into Lagos, the former capital of Nigeria to be identified with modernism which the new language, English has created.

In examining the Nigerians attitudes towards the English language, attempt is made to consider the link between a language and the combined factors of social identity, culture and individuality.

Evolution of English in Nigeria

The evolution of English language in Nigeria has been traced by Alabi (1994) to pre trans-Atlantic slave trade era, specifically in 1553 when some British were said to have paid what Alabi described as —very brief visits to the Nigerian coasts especially the ports of Benin and old Calabarǁ. The first obstacle confronted by the visitors was communication barrier between the natives and the English men. There was then a pressing need to dislodge this obstruction, hence, the need to teach the Basic English for communication, business transaction, missionary activities and for other official functions.

At the initial stage, the medium of communication between the English men and the natives was English-based pidgin. Since the traders, missionaries and colonial administrators were not willing to learn the indigenous language(s), English had to be imposed and taught in order to train clerks, interpreters, stewards, messengers to help white men in administrative and domestic activities.

It is therefore evident that the cornerstone of the British introduction of the teaching of English Language was not based on evolution of a standard English but on the emergence of a fairly communicative English. Therefore, right from the onset, there has been a basis for dialectal varieties in Nigeria spoken English.

Candidature of the English Language

Bamgbose (1987) observes that —the question whether there is a Nigerian English (as a variety of world Englishes) should at this point have become a non-issue, given the need for its interactional and transactional roles in a multi-lingual context like Nigeria.

Lending weight to traces of ethnic markers in the spoken English of an average Nigerian, Bamgbose stresses that when two languages come into contact and one is performing an official role, such language will be influenced both culturally and linguistically in accordance with the reciprocal influence theory of language variation.

Thus, Nigerian English has come to stay as long as the official status of English in the Nigerian society is sustained. Many characteristic features of Nigerian dialectal forms of the English language exist at the syntactic, semantic, pragmatic and linguistic levels. Interestingly, these ethnic traits do not simply disappear just because a speaker is educated. This is because variation in English reveals more of cultural difference. The language, as it is now, has been domesticated' to reflect the general social context within which it functions.

Attitudes towards the English Language

Adegbija (1994) quoted Fitch and Hopper as defining language attitude simply as —the evaluative judgment about others' speech patterns. In other words, it is the evaluative judgment made about language (or its variety) and its speakers feared towards promoting, maintaining or planning of language, or even towards learning and teaching of language. He described attitudes as complex phenomena —which could be observable or internal, or both simultaneously, temporary or lasting, and of surface levels of deep-rooted nature.

Nigerians' attitude towards the status and use of the English language is ambivalent. This incompatibility in the attitude is due to the close affinity a language shares with the mind and culture. It is therefore evident that the cornerstone of the British introduction of the teaching of English language was not based on evolution of a "standard" English but on the emergence of a fairly communicative English. Therefore, right from say (1987) observes that —the question whether there is a Nigerian English (as a variety of world Englishes) should at this point. English, apart from the role assigned to play, also becomes subservient to cultural milieu and its worldview. Variables like culture, worldview, among others, can affect the externalization or codification of thought(s) which a language conveys. Also, variables like religion, ideology, environment (where perhaps the speakers attend school), tribal chauvinism and its accent, considerably affect the production of sounds, use of expressions and choice of words. This is because according to Ofuokwu: (1990).

It is expected that members of an ethnic group seeking social and psycholinguistic distinctiveness (Giles, Bourhis and Tailor 1977) will invariably accentuate the ethnic markers in their speech by exhibiting remarkable speech divergence instead of —convergence‖.

Since ethnic rivalry persists in Nigerian context, many ethnic groups think it is by speaking English marked by ethnosyncracies that their social identity can be safeguarded.

The speakers in this context can fit into what Odumuh categorized as Educated Nigerian English in his typology of the Nigerian English. (Odmuh, 1998). Nigerians express very strong and positive feelings of loyalty for their indigenous languages because of their relevance to cultural and national identity. So every bit of ethnic manifestation is done sometimes deliberately and with pride. A cursory examination of ambivalent attitude towards the use of English in Nigeria can be simplified further by classifying the society into Micro and Macro societies. Micro includes federal institutions and academic environment while Macro comprises the larger societies, local or state based gatherings.

In the former, the speaking of the English language wins confidence, respect, dignity and aura of glorification for the speakers from the audience the degree of which got increased if it devoid ethnic markers. The latter represents the socio-political order and is characterized by divergent audience whose appetite for the use of English is based on socio-cultural canon. To this group, dialectal English is at par with the so-called standard English because, after all, English is principally needed for inter-personal communication, thus —nothing more, as Soyinka (1977) observes, —(other) than tool for convenience….

Defining the vitality of ethnologuistic group, Ofuokwu quoted Giles et. al. (1979) as saying that it is —that which makes a group likely to behave as a distinctive and active collective entity in inter-grouping situations‖. He further includes identity status, demography and institutional support as being supportive to ethnic vitality.

Precisely, of all the three major tribes in Nigeria, Hausa seems to be the least that attaches great importance or exerts pressure on itself in speaking British Standard English. This underscores the value attached to the duo factors of ethnicity and religion. The Hausa people do not only regard their language as a primus interpares among the Nigerian languages but also see the English language as a language of Christianity. The language is also often seen as a language of the foreigners who have come to subdue our cultural and religious institutions. More so, due to the fact that the tribe has featured or produced more political leaders in Nigeria than any other tribe, the speaking of Hausa dialectical English enjoins more recognition among many Hausa top government officials and some of their academics than other varieties. No serious attempt has been made to adopt the Received Pronunciation other than those meant for academic purpose. This variety is also favored by the demographic strength, which ensures the highest numerical distribution of speakers throughout the country.

However, all the major tribes nurture different varieties and are mostly proud of them because of what —core values‖ have come to represent in socio-political system in Nigeria. Ndukwe defines core values as —those values that are regarded as forming the most fundamental components of a group culture‖. These, according to him, are considered the representation of —the heartland of the ideological system‖ and they are symbolic of the group they represent.

In addition to the foregoing discussion on ethnic influence on the English language, the user's communicative competence also has a role to play. The low level of education, exposure and inter-ethnic interaction also promotes the lackadaisical attitude of Nigerians towards attaining a standard form of Nigeria English.

Moreover, the few academic moves that have been made towards eradicating what is usually considered non-standard or dialectal English is often seen as shying away from a linguistic reality. Such perpetrators are, according to Alladina and Edwards (1991) —…guilty of under-estimating the potency of language (including the varieties) as a symbol of identity.

In the Eastern part of the country, the influence of Pidgin English is highly noticeable. Pidgin, for long, has been adopted as a language of inter-ethnic communication. As a result, the freedom enjoyed in the speaking of pidgin is hereby transferred to the real English language already characterized by ethnic markers.

It should be noted that such ethnic influences are inevitable, and indeed necessary. What ethnicity and its concomitant variables tried to do is to domesticate English language for Nigerians' convenient use.

It is also observed that the natives often reluctantly or/and cautiously use Standard English. This is because the natives perceive the so-called standard form as being too formalistic and totally foreign to the Nigerians. This lack of respect syndrome is illustrative at the lexico-semantic level. For instance, in Yoruba, lexes like —Eyin and —Won, apart from being pluralistic can equally be used in singular sense to convey a referential tone in their semantic implication.

As a result of this complexity, speakers often to code-mixing. This tends to make the speakers feel at home without much attention paid to the grammatical formations.

One must equally recognized the influence of the mother tongue which serves as the pioneer language through which a child first learns to express his thoughts, feelings and experience. The English language, against this backdrop, is then viewed as not having enough expressive resources that can match any of the native languages. Since in Nigeria, mostly in Macro Society and sometimes in Micro Society (in the typologies earlier mentioned), speakers, in their daily interaction, make use of their first language. This practice has turned part and parcel of the natives who now consider it tasking to use a foreign expression called Standard English. In this regard, the English language is viewed contemptuously as a colonial stigma. Jowitt (1991) observes that most Nigerians often argue against the use of English as being a

—Language imported into Nigeria from Europe and therefore not the language in which Nigerians express their inner most thoughts…. English is an instrument of imperialism…. (and) should be replaced by an African language.

Therefore, the best way out of this quagmire is a dialectal English which its native speakers can maneuver proverbs and idioms available, for example, in their tribal language to externalize their thoughts almost perfectly.

Dialectal English in Nigeria is also used to establish a form of informal conversational context. Speakers feel relaxed, original and natural while speaking it than when speaking rule-studded English.

One thing is however crystal clear that in spite of all the foregoing sentiments, the English language remains the only strong cord that binds Nigeria and Nigerians together irrespective of the country's multi-cultural, multi-lingual and multi-ethnic differences. English has continued to function against all odds in various domains of life.

Characteristics of Dialectal English in Nigeria

As long as the human impulse to have a uniquely distinctive socio-cultural identity thrives, language will continue to be as diverse as those who speak it. It is these socio-cultural traits that sometimes turn to a source of worry for linguists as they seek legitimacy for such language.

Adegbija (1998) observes and gives a list of what he termed problems arising in the use of the English Language in Nigeria. In the context of this paper and the researcher's view, they can be called the characteristics of Nigerian Dialectal English. Adegbija's observation are summarized below. That such English:

1.   Could be generally intelligible but ungrammatical. For instance, can you please off the light

2.   Could be meaningful in Nigerian context only. For instance small by small the small man becomes a big man.

3.   Could be grammatical but adjudged hypercorrect thus rendering the statement socially unacceptable. For instance, in requesting, some might say: Would you please help me lift this load?

4.   Could be internationally unacceptable but locally intelligible. E.g How work?, How now?.

5.   Finally, it could be deviant according to native speaker norms but often unacceptable locally. For instance; ―Sorry‖ (as an expression of sympathy for an incident not caused by the speaker)

Certain features in indigenous languages are being transferred directly into the

Nigerian English. This socio-linguistic variable considerably helps cement or consolidate social interaction.

For instance, the forms of greeting like —Well done‖ and —Well seated are commonly used. The concept of the former has been extended and made relevant to encompass certain situation not originally intended in the Standard English while the latter is a Nigerian coined lexis carried to be an English equivalent of the one in indigenous languages.

While the use of —well done‖ in Nigerian context is a form of greeting used as a casual greeting by a passerby for the workers on a job or who have satisfactorily completed a job, —well seated‖ is used to acknowledge the presence of those who are in sitting position as at the time the speaker is passing by.

Usually —well seated‖ is used by the speaker to pay homage to those he meets sitting before he proceeds to ask for a favor.

Nigerians are fond of these greetings, according to Prof. Funsho Akere (1981) —because the English language does not possess linguistic markers for such non-occurring features, the Nigerian user of English substitutes the nearest equivalents in English for them.

Similarly, average Nigerian speakers of the English use the expression —I am coming‖ in a peculiar context. Generally, Nigerians say —I am coming‖ when they are actually going. This is so, because such expression is available in the three major languages.

For instance Hausa says —Ina Zuwa‖, Ibo —Anamabia‖ and Yoruba —Mo nbo (wa). Therefore, Nigerians found the English expression —I am coming‖ as a suitable and relevant equivalent, thus the cause of the direct translation from the mother tongue.

Let us consider the following common expressions in the Nigerian English and see how they are arrived at.

Nigerians common expressions and their Hausa Igbo and Yoruba geneses respectively

i. I want to give you a message (I have a message for you) = Zan bada sako

ii. I want to enter taxi (I want to board a taxi) = Ina so in shiga mota

iii. I want to do marriage (I want to organize a marriage Ceremony) = Ina so in yiaure

(i)   He has brain (He is intelligent/brilliant) = O nwereuburu

(ii)   It is good the way you came now (it is good that you have come/it is good that you are present) = O dinma etu isiri biaugbua

(iii)   My stomach is paining me (I have a stomach upset) = Afo naa him

(iv)   My mother bought me market things (My mother bought me some things (items)from the market) = Nnem Zuru lami heahia

(i)   I came down from the motor (I alighted from the motor) = Mo so kale ninu oko naa.

(ii)   Call me Jide (Call Jide for me) = Bami pe Jide

(iii)   They are calling you (You are called) Won npe o.

Also co-existing with the ethnic–marked English language in Nigeria is the pidgin. In the pidgin, many ethnic markers are featured more easily at all its structural _levels, many times direct indigenous lexes are used.

As earlier observed in this paper, the pride and importance attached with the English language-based pidgin is so great that even in the eastern part of the country, it is the pidgin or broken English and not the Igbo language that serves as the predominant language of communication. It even provides for them a regional lingua franca considering the diverse ethno-linguistic set-up of the region. It is also interesting that the Igbos as well as a good number of other-tribes (minor or major) use dialectal or ethnic marked English language not only at the grass root level but also in some formal events dominated by the speaker(s) tribe.

The degree of attachment demonstrated by both Igbo and Yoruba to the English language differs from that of Hausa-Fulani ethnic group. The patronage of English among the core-northerners is the least. Apart from the aforementioned sentiments on the ground, it is also the last region to have a taste of western education. On the Nigerian political scene, Hausa language is in the forefront among the indigenous languages contending for national or official status coupled with a long political dominance that lends more advantage to the socio-linguistic relevance attached to this language.

Conversely, in the western part of Nigeria, the use of Standard English is accorded utmost respect. Thus, it is evidently common to see interlocutors of the same Yoruba origin using English as a medium of communication whether in formal or informal situation. This does not however erase those ethnic traits known with Yoruba in their verbal discourse.

Conclusion

This research work has tried to launch a campaign against the discriminatory and Segregationist posture of the Nigerians in general against their languages and cultures. It advocates that in spite of the social changes coming forth, there should not be neglect of our languages and cultures which could pose tribal and foreign clashes in the future.

The influence of English language on our indigenous language cannot be over looked. It is the most important heritage left by the British colonialists as a unifying force, but that does not mean that we should de-emphasize our indigenous languages in their own functional domains. From the data collected, English language has a negative influence on our indigenous languages. This is because, all the functions meant to be performed by our indigenous languages have been taken over by English language because of the purported integration it fosters. And most importantly is the issue of borrowing of English into our vocabularies. From our data, we noticed that most students cannot communicate fluently in their mother tongue without adding one or two English vocabularies to their mother tongue. This is a bad influence on our indigenous languages, because as a result of borrowings from English language; it is only aiding the growth of English but leading to the death of our own indigenous languages. The negative influence of English language on our Nigerian indigenous languages have taken prime or dominance and above, then in terms of academic instructional materials in schools. In contrast with the Nigeria language policy which stipulate that the three major indigenous Nigerian languages which are Hausa, Igbo and Yoruba should be used as a media of instruction at the early stages of primary education, English has taken over this functional role, that is English is now used in relatively all levels of Nigerian educational system.

Another instance of those negative effects comes from the mass-media. It is obvious that in Nigerian mass media, English is mostly used at the expense of our indigenous languages. Therefore, owing to the fact that many a time, they do not have access to vital information since the information are not disseminated in their native languages.

This concept of the inseparable linkages between language, society and culture, which ensure economic subsistence of society, is important in a consideration of the social and cultural impact of English as International Language, because EIL concerns the relationship between the international spread of English across national boundaries and the many groups of people within their own societies, each with distinct traditional languages and ethnic traditions, since the beginning of colonialism around 500 years ago, to the present age of globalization.

Phillipson (1992, 166) views the spread of EIL as repressive since it not only substitutes and displaces other languages, but also imposes new _mental structures' on learners (please see the appendix). These _mental structures' are possibly the ideologies that Westerners use to justify their own culture and impose these ideas on others. He sees English learning and culture as inseparable, given that he sees

_modernization' and _nation building' as being _a logical process of English Language Teaching'.

Phillipson also considers the implications of this, and criticizes the English language teaching (ELT) profession for not having cross-cultural studies as part of its core, and for not having any principled consideration for the educational consequences that follow from its own awareness of this situation, thereby implying that ELT is not only ignorant, but also guilty, of the _linguistic imperialism' it promotes.

Culture would seem to be as important to communication as it is to personal identity, and the two are related to economic subsistence as the prime consideration, thus colonization aimed to destroy the personal identity of the colonized. It had to subdue their resistance by marginalizing, among others, their indigenous channels of communication and forcing them to learn English, the language of the colonizer.

This would seem why, as Phillipson points out, English learning and culture are inseparable, and the imposition of Western ways of thinking (_modernization' and _nation building') are _a logical process of ELT', in the same way that economic inequality, sustained by EIL through ELT, was a logical process of colonization, in order to keep the poor nations economically poor, mentally subdued, and hence easily exploitable.

However, the role of ELT and EIL has also changed somewhat since that time. They have become somewhat more sensitive in their interaction with other cultures, while English has become adopted as a part of the culture of many former non-English speaking countries. There is a growing realization that EIL is becoming adopted by people who speak it as a second language, and not as something being imposed from the outside anymore. Crystal (1992) noted that non-native speakers of English represent more than two-thirds of its potential speakers. Swales (1993, 284) emphasized that:

…internationalism favors no nation nor gives any permanent credit for the length of membership in a global association. Therefore we have to concede that it no longer makes any sense to differentiate between the native speaker and the non-native speaker.

Similarly Walker (2001, 1) reports that:

English is currently regarded as the world's principal international language. As a result there are now more exchanges between non-native speakers of English than between non-native speakers and native speakers. In the immediate future at least, this situation is unlikely to change in favour of the minority of native speakers, and so suddenly the hegemony of their particular (and sometimes peculiar) accents is under fire.

Kramsch and Sullivan (1996, 199) note that:

The notion of —authentic‖ becomes problematic within the framework of English as an international language: whose words and whose culture comprise authentic language?

Thus, it could be fair to say that English no longer belongs to any particular group of people, and that they are no longer mere consumers of the Western-Anglo-Saxon tradition. Kachru (1982, cited by Talebinezhad and Aliakbari, 2001, 1), despite his predominant focus on the unbalanced center-periphery relationship, admitted that ‗for the first time a natural language has attained the status of an international (universal) language'. Kachru (1994, 135) also saw English as being very adaptable and thus capable of sustaining a large assortment of functions. It seems that this phenomenon of EIL, the adoption and ownership of English by formally non-English speaking societies, is a major switch in the role of EIL from its former repressive role, to one that offers possibilities for EIL being used in a liberating sense.

In conclusion, the influence of English Language on Nigerian Languages and Cultures seem to be a controversial issue because it has come to stay in the country among the people. It will keep on having greater force on all aspects because of its unique attachment to science and technology. Nevertheless, attention should be given to the local languages, so that they will not go out of use. One's language is one's identity and the crown of one's culture. A foreign language like English among diverse languages poses no feeling and it is void of affection among second speakers unlike a native language. It should be a temporary language for communication only and a switch code method should be in vogue.

This research work is the contribution of intellectuals who feel Nigerian Languages need not die and be replaced with a foreign language that can cause disunity out of misuse.

Bibliography

1. Adegbija, E. E. (1994) Language Attitudes in sub-Saharan Africa: A socio linguistic Overview. Clevedon Avon: Multilingual matters.

*2..*Aboh, Enoch O. "Topic and Focus within D". *Linguistics in The Netherlands 21: 1-12, 2004.*

Bamgbose, Ayo. "English in the Nigerian Environment". Ayo Bamgbose et al. (eds.). *New*
Englishes: A West African Perspective. Ibadan: Mosuro, 1995.

3. AkereFunso (1981) ―Socio-cultural Constraints and The Emergence of Standard Nigerian English in The Nigerian Language Teacher Lagos, National Language Center.Vol. 4 No 1.

4. Alabi, V.A. (1994) ―English Language in Second Language Context‖ OluObafemi (ed). The English Language in Nigeria, Ibadan, Oluseyi Press.

5. AlladinaSafder and Edwards Viv (1991) Multilingualism in the British Isles 2 Africa, the Middle East and Asia. London, Longman.

6. Bamgbose, Ayo (1982), ―Standard Nigerian English - issue of identification‖. The other Tongue‖ Urbana, University of Illinois Press.

7. Chumbow, Sammy (1990) ―The Place of The Mother Tongue in the National Policy on Education‖ Emenanjo E.N. (ed) Multilingualism in Minority Languages and Language Policy in Nigeria. Central Books Limited.

8. Jowitt David (1991) Nigeria English Usage – An Introduction Ikeja Longman.

9. Littlewood William (1984) Foreign and Second Language Learning. New York Cambridge University Press

10. Odumuh, A. E. (1987) Nigerian English. Zaria ABU Press.

11. Odumuh, A. E. (1989) ―The Co-existence of English and Nigerian Languages‖ in Ilorin Journal of Language and Literature, Department of Modern European Languages, University of Ilorin.

12. Ofuokwu, Dili (1990) ―Socio-linguistic Variety and Language Planning: The

Nigerian situation‖. Emnanjo E.N. (ed) Multilingualism in Minority Languages and Language Policy in Nigeria. Central Books Limited.

13. Soyinka, Wole (1977) —Language As Boundary‖ in Language Education in Nigerian Vol. 1

14. AdebilejeAdebola, OlusolaOdebode, Mark Ighile, AdeniyiAdeleke An Appraisal of the Effectiveness of Mother Tongue as Medium of Teaching in Selected Primary Schools in Nigeria.

15. Phillipson, R (1992) Linguistic Impreialism. Oxford: Oxford University Press.

16. Phillipson, R (1992) Linguistic Impreialism. Oxford: Oxford University Press.

17. Abbott, G. (1989) ‗Should we start digging new holes?' In Kennedy, C. et al (2001)

18. Sociolinguistics.Center for English Language Studies, Birmingham University, pp.97-98.

19. Abbott, G. (1992) ‗Development, education, and English language teaching.'ELT Journal 46/2: 172-178.

20. Crystal, D. (1997) English as a Global Language. Cambridge: Cambridge University Press.

APPENDIX

RESEARCH WORK CONDUCTED IN THE DEPARTMENT OF ENGLISH
REDEEMER'S UNIVERSITY
MOWE OGUN STATE
NIGERIA
TOPIC: ENGLISH LANGUAGE IN A MULTILINGUAL
SOCIETY
RESEARCHER: DR. JANE LANDEY
CLASS IN FOCUS: 300 LEVEL
LECTURER IN CHARGE: DR. A. O. ADEBILEJE

QUESTIONAIRE

Name in full:………………………………………………………..

Name of university:…………………………………………………

Name of language:………………………………………………….

What dialect do you speak in your language?...

Write the following with translation in English

Write five nouns in your language……………………………………….

Write five verbs in your language………………………………………

Write five adverbs in your language……………………………………….

Write five adjectives in your language…………………………………

Write five pronouns in your language………………………………….

Write five determiners in your language………………………………….

Write a sentence in your language in all the conjugation forms.

……………………………………………………………………………...

....

....

....

....

How has English Language affected your language?

....

In what way do you think your language should be preserved or
modified to correlate with the influence of English Language?

....
.

Or how can a native speaker be well understood by the speaker of English
Language when they come in contact with each other? E.g. come /COM/
by a Nigerian speaker instead of come /C/\M/ by a British person.

....

What are the norms in your culture that you admire so much?

....

What similarity (ies) has your language in terms of grammatical structure?

....

What difference(s) has your language in terms of grammatical function in
some way?

....

In your own view as a second language speaker of English Language, should a language in your country be adopted as the official and commercial language?

....

If so, which..

If not how should our languages and cultures be preserved to avoid odd cultural interference and degradation from this foreign language?

....

www.ingramcontent.com/pod-product-compliance
Lightning Source LLC
Chambersburg PA
CBHW081850280526
45789CB00007B/2645